TITANIC
LIVES

MW00441901

TITANIC LIVES
ON BOARD, DESTINATION CANADA

ROB RONDEAU

FORMAC PUBLISHING COMPANY LIMITED
HALIFAX

For Donna and Dylan

Copyright © 2012 by Rob Rondeau

All rights reserved. No part of this book may be reproduced or transmitted in any form or by any means, electronic or mechanical, including photocopying, or by any information storage or retrieval system, without permission in writing from the publisher.

Formac Publishing Company Limited recognizes the support of the Province of Nova Scotia through the Department of Communities, Culture and Heritage. We are pleased to work in partnership with the Culture Division to develop and promote our culture resources for all Nova Scotians. We acknowledge the financial support of the Government of Canada through the Canada Book Fund for our publishing activities. We acknowledge the support of the Canada Council for the Arts which last year invested $24.3 million in writing and publishing throughout Canada.

Canada Council   Conseil des Arts
for the Arts   du Canada

Library and Archives Canada Cataloguing in Publication

Rondeau, Rob
    Titanic lives : on board, destination Canada / Rob Rondeau.
Includes bibliographical references and index.

Also issued in electronic format.
ISBN 978-1-4595-0019-8

    1. Titanic (Steamship). 2. Titanic (Steamship)–Biography.
3. Shipwreck victims–Biography. 4. Shipwrecks–North Atlantic Ocean. I. Title.

G530.T6R65 2012   910.9163'4   C2011-908274-8

Formac Publishing Company Limited
5502 Atlantic Street
Halifax, NS, Canada
B3H 1G4
www.formac.ca

Printed in China.

CONTENTS

FOREWORD

Titanic is a great international story of drama and hubris but has often been viewed as a largely British or American story. Canada is, in fact, a big part of the *Titanic* story: the Canadian coastline in whose waters she sank, the Canadian recovery of her victims, the many Canadians aboard. As Rob Rondeau reminds us, some of the most expensive cabins aboard the grand but tragic liner were occupied by Canadians, some of whose names — Harry Molson, Charles Hays and Major Peuchen — were household names at home and abroad. These wealthy Canadians, along with those of humbler origins, whom Rob Rondeau includes in his narrative, found themselves at the centre of the key dramas and controversies that unfolded as the ship sank in epic fashion.

Titanic also plays a linked role with two great Canadian disasters. Only two years later, Canada had its own ocean liner tragedy when the Canadian Pacific Liner *Empress of Ireland* sank in the St. Lawrence River in 1914. Claiming nearly as many lives as *Titanic* but with much less recognition, the *Empress* tragedy was quickly forgotten amidst the eruption of the First World War. In 1917, just five years after the sinking of *Titanic*, Halifax was devastated by the Halifax Explosion, a munitions accident that killed almost two thousand people. Halifax had played the central role in recovering and identifying *Titanic* victims, and the same system developed to identify *Titanic* victims was put to use to identify Canadians killed by this even larger disaster.

Titanic has certainly inspired Canadian writers, starting with Canadian poet E. J. Pratt, who wrote a sweeping epic poem, *The Titanic*, in 1935. Canadian oceanographer Richard Brown was perhaps the first to explore *Titanic*'s Canadian geographic connection in his 1983 book, *The Voyage of the Iceberg*, which uniquely told of the sinking from the iceberg's point of view. Another ocean scientist, Alan Ruffman, brought these threads together in his telling of the sinking and the recovery of victims in his 1999 book, *Titanic Remembered: The Unsinkable Ship and Halifax*, while Alan Hustak's 1998 book, *Titanic: The Canadian Story*, was the first to explore the many Canadians lives aboard the ship.

When we created the exhibit *Titanic: The Unsinkable Ship and Halifax* at the Maritime Museum of the Atlantic in 1997, we were eager to identify the fascinating but little-known Canadians who had boarded the doomed ship. Thanks to help from authors Hustak and Ruffman, we illustrated the lives in first class of Helene Baxter, the widow of a Montreal financier, and the apple of her eye, her son Quigg. Our window into second class was Alfred Pain, a young doctor from Hamilton who was top of his class at the University of

Toronto; he had planned to return home as a doctor on a tramp steamer but ended up aboard *Titanic*.

With his welcome look at more of the Canadians aboard *Titanic*, Rob Rondeau re-introduces many of these people in far more detail than our museum could present in an exhibit. Rob, an underwater archaeologist, has been planning work to document *Titanic*'s wreck; that has given him a special interest in the Canadians whose cabins he hopes someday to explore. Rondeau connects their lives and experience with the construction, outfitting and accommodations of the ship around them. The stories he tells reveal the rich and complicated lives of *Titanic* victims and survivors. In many cases, odd twists of fate in seemingly innocent decisions or unpredictable circumstances led them to book passage on the doomed liner.

Some of those passengers were rich in money, while others were rich with experiences ranging from Klondike gold mining to Boer War battles and adventures in the worlds of fine art, high society and big business. Some of the personal stories, notably that of Quigg Baxter and his secret love affair with a dance hall girl, or the bitter and heartbreaking story of the Allison family who frantically searched for their daughter as the ship sank, seem right out of a movie. They remind us that real life can be every bit as melodramatic as a Hollywood blockbuster.

The range of people aboard *Titanic* is perhaps one of the most compelling features of the story of this shipwreck. In the saga of death and survival that night we can all find someone to identify with, people of all ages from the very rich to the very poor. Charles Hays was a Canadian railway tycoon who built much of Canada's travel infrastructure, and our museum has long displayed his fine leather gloves, which were found with his body and kept by local undertakers. They are now displayed beside the shoes found on the body of two-year-old Sidney Goodwin, who died along with his entire family in third class. The gloves of a millionaire and the shoes of a working-class toddler remind us all of the many lives brought together in tragic fashion aboard *Titanic*.

— Dan Conlin, Curator, Maritime Museum of the Atlantic
August 2011

INTRODUCTION

You might say that this book has been thirty years in the making! I first learned of *Titanic* when I was thirteen years old and I've been fascinated with its story ever since. This fascination shaped my adult life. First I became a scuba diver, then I studied archaeology. My love of *Titanic* has fuelled my career, and life-long adventure, as a marine archaeologist.

When I first considered writing a book about the late great liner in conjunction with the one hundredth anniversary of its sinking, I knew that I wanted to focus on stories that hadn't been told before.

Also, I wanted the book to be uniquely Canadian. All of the ten main characters were destined for somewhere across this country. Some were native sons and daughters of the great Dominion, some were transplants and some were coming here for the first time. Their lives were as varied as Canada is vast.

I deliberately chose not to focus on the technical aspects of *Titanic* itself and its sinking. There are already many excellent books that have done this. Rather, I have tried to "set the scene," so to speak, to give the reader a better view of what it would have been like aboard ship for each of the ten.

The scene itself is also larger than just *Titanic*. I have tried to pull back the curtain, exposing what it would have been like to have lived at the beginning of the twentieth century.

Rob Rondeau
Marine Archaeologist
Lunenburg, Nova Scotia
September 2011

PAUL CHEVRE
Haunted to Death

Chevre was the closest thing to a celebrity artist at the time. In many ways, his short life reflected the equally brief, but spectacular, Edwardian era.

He was born in Brussels to French parents in 1867. His father managed a foundry there. As a boy, Chevre showed an interest in sculpture.

When he was twenty-three, Chevre exhibited his work for the first time at the Paris International Exhibition, the "Exposition Universelle," of 1889. It was held to mark the 100th anniversary of the storming of the Bastille, which, in turn, marked the beginning of the French Revolution.

The highlight of the exhibition was the new Eiffel Tower, which had been constructed the year before. It served as the entrance arch to the fair.

Prominent visitors to the world's fair included Britain's Prince of Wales, the future King Edward VII (for whom the "Edwardian Era" was named),

French composer Claude Debussy, artists Paul Gauguin and Vincent van Gogh and American inventor Thomas Edison. Famed American sharpshooter Annie Oakley was the star attraction of Buffalo Bill's Wild West Show and performed to packed audiences daily.

Six years later, Chevre won the commission to produce a monumental sculpture of Canada's founder, Samuel de Champlain. It stands in Quebec City on the Dufferin Terrace beside the Chateau Frontenac Hotel. Art critics at the time, and art historians since, consider it Chevre's best work. The statue of Champlain was dedicated on September 21, 1898, by Canada's then governor general, Lord Aberdeen.

In 1900, Chevre won the bronze medal for sculpture at the second Paris International Exhibition. Held on the same site as the 1889 exhibition, the world's fair was held to celebrate the achievements of the past century. A new name, "Art Nouveau," was coined to express the Exhibition's style.

At only thirty-three years of age, Chevre was an international art superstar. From then on, his work was in high demand, especially with Canada's "Nouveau Riche." He spent half of each year in Montreal, wining and dining would-be patrons. The other half of the year he spent sculpting in his studio located on the outskirts of Paris.

In 1909, Chevre was commissioned to create a statue of then Quebec premier Honoré Mercier. It stands on the grounds of the Quebec Legislature. In 1911, he was commissioned to create a statue of the famed Canadian historian, Francois-Xavier Garneau.

Chevre planned to return to Canada by train after arriving in New York aboard *Titanic*. He boarded the liner at Cherbourg, France, as a first-class passenger. He paid twenty-nine pounds, fourteen shillings, for his ticket.

Chevre had the reputation of being an excitable and nervous traveller. As a result, he had booked stateroom A-9, on *Titanic*'s upper promenade deck. Located one deck below the bridge, he had been assured by the White Star Line that it was one of the safest cabins on the ship.

The days leading up to *Titanic*'s sinking were uneventful for Chevre. Without question, he made a point to visit with the president of the Grand Trunk Pacific Railway, Charles Hays, and his wife, Clara. Hays's railroad had commissioned Chevre to create a bust of then prime minister Sir Wilfrid Laurier for the lobby of its newest hotel, the Chateau Laurier Hotel in Ottawa. It remains one of Canada's premier hotels and is located across the street from the nation's parliament buildings.

The hotel was due to open on April 26, 1912,

Samuel de Champlain statue.

11

and Chevre, ever the celebrity, planned to be there for his sculpture's unveiling.

That fateful Sunday night, April 14, when *Titanic* hit the iceberg that sealed its fate, Chevre was playing bridge in the ship's Café Parisien with three other first-class passengers, two fellow Frenchmen and an American.

Even though things didn't appear to be serious at first, the card players soon got up from their game and went to investigate. They watched as crewmen removed the tarp covering Lifeboat Number Seven and prepared to lower it away.

When they called for passengers, Chevre and the other Frenchmen didn't hesitate. Some other first-class passengers who were milling about on the boat deck chided the men for getting into the lifeboat, saying that it was just a false alarm. Regardless, Chevre wasn't taking any chances.

Their lifeboat was the first to depart at 12:45 a.m., April 15, roughly one hour after *Titanic* had hit the iceberg. It was less than half full.

Chevre's story was later told in the *New York Times*'s Saturday edition, April 20, 1912. Part of it read:

We were quietly playing auction bridge with a Mr. Smith from Philadelphia (who didn't survive), when we heard a violent noise similar to that produced by the screw racing. We were startled and looked at one another under the impression that a serious accident had happened.

We did not, however, think for a catastrophe, but through the portholes we saw ice rubbing against the ship's side. We rushed on deck and saw that the Titanic *had a tremendous list.*

There was everywhere a momentary panic, but it speedily subsided. To the inquiries of a lady one of the ship's officers caustically

replied, "Don't be afraid, we are only cutting a whale in two."

Confidence was quickly restored, all being convinced that the Titanic *could not founder. Captain Smith nevertheless appeared nervous; he came down on deck chewing a toothpick. "Let everyone," he said, "put on a lifebelt, it is more prudent."*

He then ordered the boats to be got out. The band continued to play popular airs in order to reassure the passengers. Nobody wanted to go in the boats, everyone saying "What's the use?" and firmly believing there was no risk in remaining on board. In these circumstances some of the boats went away with very few passengers; we saw boats with only about 15 persons in them.

Disregarding the advice of the officers many of the passengers continued to cling to the ship. When our boat (Number Seven) had rowed about half a mile from the vessel the spectacle was quite fairylike. The Titanic, *which was illuminated from stem to stern, was perfectly stationary, like some fantastic piece of stage scenery. The night was clear and the sea perfectly smooth, but it was intensely cold.*

Presently, the gigantic ship began to sink by the bow and then those who had remained on board realised to the full the horror of their situation. Suddenly the lights went out, and an immense clamour filled the air.

Little by little the Titanic *settled down, and for three hours cries were heard. At moments the cries were lulled, and we thought it was all over, but the next instant they were renewed in still keener accents.*

As for us, we did nothing but row and row to escape from the obsession of the heartrendering

First-class cabin similar to Chevre's

cries. One by one the voices were stilled.

Strange to say, the Titanic sank without noise and, contrary to expectations, the suction was very feeble. There was a great backwash and that was all. In the final spasm, the stern of the leviathan stood in the air and then the vessel finally disappeared — completely lost.

In our little boat we were frozen with cold, having left the ship without overcoats or rugs. We shouted from time to time to attract the attention of the other boats, but obtained no reply. A German baron [Alfred Nourney], who was with us, fired off all the cartridges in his revolver. This agonizing suspense lasted for many hours, until at last the Carpathia appeared.

We shouted "Hurrah" and all the boats scattered on the sea made towards her. For us

it was like coming back to life.

A particularly painful episode occurred on board the Titanic after all the boats had left. Some of the passengers who had remained on the ship, realizing too late that she was lost, tried to launch a collapsible boat, which they had great difficulty in getting into place.

Nevertheless they succeeded in lowering it. The frail boat was soon half full of water and the occupants, one after the other, either were drowned or perished with cold — the bodies of those who died being thrown out.

Of the original 50 only 15 were picked up by the Carpathia, on board which we joined them. We cannot praise too highly the conduct of the officers and men of the Carpathia. All her passengers gave up their cabins to the rescued women and the sick, and we were

received with every possible kindness.
Similarly, we bear sorrowful tribute
to the brave dead of the Titanic. *Colonel*
Astor and the others were admirable in their
heroism and the crew fulfilled with sublime
self-sacrifice all the dictates of humanity.
Much useless sacrifice of life would have
been avoided but for the blind faith in the
"unsinkableness" of the ship and if all the
places in the boats had been taken in time.

On his arrival in New York, Chevre was also interviewed by a reporter from the English daily newspaper, the *Montreal Herald*. However, the reporter didn't speak French. The article he wrote quoted Chevre as saying that he saw Captain Smith shoot himself in the head. "He (Capt. Smith) cried out, 'My luck has turned,' and then shot himself. I saw him fall against the canvas railing on the bridge and disappear."

The salacious story appeared not only in the *Montreal Herald* but also in several other major English newspapers on both sides of the Atlantic.

Of course, it would have been impossible for Chevre to have seen Smith commit suicide because when his lifeboat was lowered away Smith was very much alive, as witnessed by other survivors. Smith did not disappear until later that night. His body was never recovered.

The same article also said that the marble bust of Sir Wilfrid Laurier had been lost in the sinking.

On his return to his adopted city, Chevre stormed into the offices of Montreal's French language daily newspaper, *La Presse*, to set the record straight. Everything in the English article had been "a tissue of lies," he said.

In its April 22nd edition, the French newspaper published Chevre's side of the story, in which he vehemently denied seeing *Titanic*'s captain kill himself. Also, he confirmed that the Laurier sculpture was most certainly safe. In fact, it had been shipped to Montreal separately aboard another ship, the *Bertagne*.

"It weighs 7,445 pounds. How do you think I could have had it in my cabin? Good Lord!" he was quoted as saying.

Chevre remained in Canada for six months after the *Titanic*'s sinking. He obtained a commission to sculpt another statue, "Marianne," which stands today outside the Union Française building in Montreal.

Chevre is said to have suffered during the return passage by ship to France in the fall of 1912. He kept to himself, staying out of sight in his cabin most of the journey. He did not travel on the sea again, and died only two years later, at the age of forty-seven.

His Paris obituary read that he never fully recovered from the shock of that terrible night. Others claimed that he had been haunted by what he saw.

Edward VII: A Life of Excess

Edward VII's short reign, from January 22, 1901, to May 6, 1910, defined the period named after him, the "Edwardian Era," which extended from the beginning of the twentieth century until the beginning of World War I in 1914. He was the son of Queen Victoria and Prince Albert. Before ascending the throne, he held the title of Prince of Wales and was heir apparent to the throne for longer than anyone else in history, with the exception of Prince Charles today.

He was not an intellectual, despite earning an undergraduate degree from Oxford University. Britain's Prime Minister Benjamin Disraeli described him as being "informed, intelligent and of a sweet manner."

To his family and friends he was known as "Bertie." In less polite social circles, he was known as a charmer and playboy. While pledged in marriage to Alexandra, Princess of Denmark, he was romantically linked to an actress, Nellie Clifden. After he was married to Alexandra, he had many mistresses, including Winston Churchill's mother, Lady Randolph Churchill. He was an equal-opportunity philanderer, involved with noblewomen and commoners alike, even a prostitute. After his death, it was alleged that he had had as many as fifty-five lovers during his short sixty-year life.

While heir apparent, he was involved in several scandals, allegedly causing divorce between a member of parliament and his wife, as well as playing cards for money. He was also a dandy. He made wearing tweed jackets and Homburg hats fashionable, and popularized wearing a black tie with a dinner jacket instead of white tie and tails. The modern-day tradition of men not buttoning the bottom button of a suit coat or sports jacket is said to be linked to Edward, who supposedly left his undone because of his large girth. (His waistline at the time of his coronation was forty-eight inches!)

In his later years, Edward suffered several heart attacks, most likely due to his excessive life style. He died at Buckingham palace and is buried in St. George's Chapel at Windsor Castle.

Edward VII

CHARLES MELVILLE HAYS
What Might Have Been

Charles Hays was the "power CEO" of his day. The then prime minister, Sir Wilfrid Laurier, described him as a "railroad genius" and Canada's "greatest acquisition."

Born in Illinois, Hays grew up in Missouri. As a boy of seventeen he began his life-long career as a "railroad man," working as a clerk in the passenger department of the Atlantic and Pacific Railroad in St. Louis. He didn't stay long in that position, though.

He was quickly promoted, first to the railroad's audit department, and then to the office of the general superintendent. When he was only twenty-two years old, Hays became the secretary to the general manager of the sister company, the Missouri Pacific Railroad. At twenty-nine, he assumed the same position in the office of the general manager of the Wabash, St. Louis and Pacific Railway Company. Hays showed a talent for management, and developed a reputation for being thorough and efficient.

At thirty, Hays was named general manager for the Wabash Western, which included all the railroad's rail lines west of the Mississippi and those running between Chicago and Detroit. At thirty-three, he became general manager for the entire Wabash rail network. He remained in that position for six years, honing his business skills and advancing his craft. He became recognized for his "aptitude, enterprise and initiative."

When only thirty-nine years old, he resigned from his position of vice president for the Wabash system to become general manager of the Grand Trunk Railway of Canada (GTR), and moved his young family to Montreal.

However, Hays arrived in Canada during an eco-

Body of RMS Titanic *victim being picked up at sea by ship's whaler from the CS* Minia

nomic depression. All railways in the country were struggling financially, although the transcontinental Canadian Pacific Railway (CPR) was faring better than most. The GTR was heavily in debt.

Hays was brought onboard in 1896 to make major managerial changes — to "Americanize" the railway. His first task was to restructure the company's administration and operation. Instead of relying on only the recommendations of the railroad's top executives in London, Hays sought the opinions and advice of the railroad's regional managers in Canada.

He addressed issues that head office had ignored for years, such as negotiating better traffic exchanges and running rights with other railway systems. He even sold off important trackage between Toronto and Hamilton to GTR's main rival, the CPR, in exchange for better running rights on other CPR rail lines.

Hays also modernized the GTR's accounting procedures and spearheaded many other improvements. He supervised the construction of the double-track open-span bridge crossing the St. Lawrence River at Montreal, the Victoria Jubilee Bridge, which is still in use today. He also saw to the creation of a single-span steel arch bridge over the Niagara River at Niagara Falls, replacing the old suspension bridge there.

By the time Hays sailed on *Titanic*, the GTR's main line had been double-tracked all the way from Montreal to Chicago, and the railway was back in the black.

Sir Charles Wilson, GTR's president in 1896, believed that the West held the key to the railroad's success. He was right. The early twentieth century saw an unprecedented growth in immigration to

He Didn't Go Down With His Ship

Titanic's *lifeboats*

Prior to the *Titanic* disaster, J. Bruce Ismay had planned to step down as president of International Maritime Marine (IMM), the U.S. parent company of the White Star Line. He had held the position for four years.

He had hoped to stay on as White Star's chairman, but IMM's board of directors wouldn't have it. Many of them, like most of the public, felt that Ismay should have gone down with *Titanic*, his ship, when it sank on April 15, 1912.

At the time, Ismay was portrayed by the press on both sides of the Atlantic as the disaster's villain. After all, it was his company that hadn't provided enough lifeboats for everyone on board *Titanic*. The ship's captain, Edward Smith, had gone down with his ship, and

so too should have Ismay, many mused.

Some newspapers of the day alleged that it was Ismay who overrode Captain Smith's orders, ordering "full steam ahead," despite Smith knowing that there was ice in the area. Ismay, the newspapers reported, wanted to beat the *Olympic*'s Atlantic crossing record.

But both the U.S. and British boards of inquiry following the disaster fully exonerated Ismay, both for being a contributing cause of the disaster and, as well, for surviving the ship's sinking. Ismay, they reasoned, only took a seat in one of *Titanic*'s lifeboats when no other man would. His staying behind would have just meant adding another death to the list.

During the "Lord Kylsant Affair," in the early 1930s,

Davits used to lower **Titanic***'s lifeboats*

an elderly Ismay (he was then in his seventies) was asked by White Star's manager, Col. Frank Bustard, to help out, but it was too late for both Ismay and the shipping line he and his father had helped to create. On May 10, 1934, the White Star and Cunard lines formally merged.

SPEED VERSUS EFFICIENCY — A COMPARISON

White Star's *Celtic* cruised at sixteen knots (eighteen mph or thirty km/h) with 14,000 horsepower, while Cunard's *Mauritania* made twenty-four knots (twenty-eight mph or forty-four km/h) with 68,000 horsepower.

In the late nineteenth century, shipbuilders discovered that above twenty knots (twenty-three mph or thirty-seven km/h), the required additional engine power increased in logarithmic proportion. The greater a ship's speed, the more engine power it needed and the more fuel it consumed. With the coal-fired reciprocating steam engines of the period, exceeding twenty-four knots was neither cost-effective nor operationally efficient!

White Star's president, J. Bruce Ismay

19

Canada from Europe. The year after *Titanic*'s sinking, 1913, was the high-water mark for new Canadians arriving, with most making their home on the prairies.

Hays shared Sir Charles's optimism and conceived of the idea to challenge the CPR's monopoly on the West by building a second, more northern, transcontinental railroad running from Moncton, New Brunswick, to Prince Rupert, British Columbia (a distance of some 3,600 miles, or 5,800 kilometres).

Hays favoured a more northern route for several reasons. One, Alberta's Peace River Valley was opening up to farming. The Grand Trunk Pacific (GTP) would run through nearby Edmonton and serve as a staging point for new immigrants to Northern Alberta. The CPR rail line ran through Calgary to the south.

Another reason was the location of Prince Rupert, where Hays planned to put the western end of his new railroad. Hays's decision to put its terminus there was controversial, to say the least. Most of the board of directors for the parent company, GTR, favoured Vancouver, to the south, instead. After all, that's where the CPR's western terminus was and that city was quickly expanding as a major shipping port.

But Hays insisted that Prince Rupert provided a shorter route to Asia. He conceived of berthing facilities there for large ships, managing both passengers and freight to and from the Orient. In addition, he dreamed of Prince Rupert being the centre of a major tourism industry — the area is renowned for its salmon and halibut fishing.

History would prove him right. Prince Rupert's sheltered harbour is the deepest ice-free natural harbour in North America, and the third-deepest natural harbour in the world. Situated at latitude fifty-four degrees north, the harbour is the northwesternmost port in North America linked to the continent's railway network. Located on the "Great Circle Route," the port is the closest West Coast port to Asia. Most cargo ships make the crossing in only three days.

Prince Rupert's container terminal today is one of the most efficient, and busiest, facilities on the North American continent. Surging Asian trade is projected to increase container volumes there by 300 per cent in the next ten years. Plans are underway to expand the terminal, quadrupling its capacity to two million containers. A second container terminal, now in the design stages, has Prince Rupert on course to handle up to five million shipping containers by 2020.

Also, most cereal grains grown on the Canadian prairies, such as wheat and barley, are shipped worldwide through Prince Rupert's high-throughput grain terminal. Another bulk terminal there also handles coal, petroleum coke and wood pellets produced in Western Canada.

The port city's new Northland Cruise Terminal, built in 2004, now accommodates a growing number of large cruise ships calling on Prince Rupert as part of their Alaska cruise program. In 2007, nearly 100,000 passengers disembarked there to explore "where the wilderness begins."

But in Hays's day, Prince Rupert was a bust! Between 1905 and 1912 only 100 miles (160 kilometres) of track was laid east of the small fishing and logging community. Most folks at the time, especially some of GTR's board of directors, thought Hays was crazy to have chosen the remote spot.

Ottawa was in favour of another transcontinental railroad. The CPR had been built with the backing of Canada's first prime minister, Sir John A. MacDonald, and his Conservative government. By

Christmas 1902, prime minister Sir Wilfrid Laurier was fed up with the CPR and its monopoly on transportation to western destinations, especially with that part of the country's rapidly growing population (and potential Liberal voters). Hays sold Laurier on the idea of an alternate rail line.

In October 1903, Canada's National Transcontinental Railway Act was passed by parliament and, soon after, work began on the new railroad. Early the next year, Hays was made president of the fledging GTP railway. While its parent company, GTR, agreed to build the line west of Winnipeg, Laurier's Liberal government assumed responsibility for constructing the line from Winnipeg to Moncton.

The turning of the sod for the construction of the new Grand Trunk Pacific rail line took place on September 11, 1905, at Fort William, Ontario, with Prime Minister Laurier doing the ceremonial digging. Charles Hays, of course, was on hand and couldn't have been prouder.

A big "man's man," he had the reputation for being jovial and good-natured, but when it came to business, he was unwilling to tolerate any interference in the way he ran things. For example, he was known to have had "implacable disdain" for organized labour, as demonstrated during a dispute in Ontario in 1905 and a bitter system-wide strike in 1910.

Cabinet was divided over a second transcontinental railroad from the start. Repeated cost overruns and the GTP's persistent demands for more money from Ottawa wore thin with many, both in cabinet and outside of it.

Nor did Hays have the unqualified support of GTR's board of directors back in London. Many were concerned by its expensive expansion into Western Canada, and some alleged that Hays had overcommitted the railway in its deal with Laurier's government. This time he may have finally gone too far, some board members mused.

Even so, when Sir Charles Wilson retired in October 1909, Hays replaced him as president of GTR. Hays was now in charge of both railroads. At that time, he was arguably one of the most influential and powerful men in Canada. The following year, he was offered a knighthood by the king of England, but he declined because doing so would have meant having to give up his U.S. citizenship.

Hays decided that the best course of action for the GTP was to spend his way out of financial trouble. He planned to compete with the CPR head-on — not only by offering an expanded railroad route, but by upgrading the GTP's rolling stock and building a chain of luxury hotels along the way. The railway's flagship hotel, the Chateau Laurier in Ottawa, was due to open on April 26, 1912, and Hays had plans to build six more hotels, including the Fort Garry Hotel in Winnipeg and the Hotel MacDonald in Edmonton.

A big problem, though, was that GTP's main line, arguably a better route across Western Canada than the CPR's, didn't then have the feeder network of smaller rail lines needed to support it. As a result, it wasn't yet profitable.

Hays had planned to spend the Easter holiday of 1912 in Paris with his wife, his daughter Orian and his son-in-law Thornton Davidson. However, when Hays and his wife learned that one of their other three daughters, Louise, was experiencing a difficult pregnancy back in Canada, they decided to return home ahead of schedule.

One of the people Hays planned to see in England before heading to Paris was J. Bruce Ismay, managing director of the White Star Line. Hays envisioned a merger between their respective companies.

Montreal's Victoria Bridge was built by the Grand Trunk Pacific Railroad under Charles Hays's direction

The CPR operated its own line of "Empress Class" passenger liners. By combining the GTP with White Star's "Olympic Class" ships, Hays was confident that his railway would be able to outclass the CPR in every way — better route, fancier hotels and more magnificent passenger ships. In return, the White Star Line would also become more competitive, being able to offer transportation from Europe to the Orient via Canada.

When Ismay learned of Hays's plans to cut short his stay in Europe, he invited Hays and his entourage to be his guests aboard White Star's newest ship, *Titanic*, on its maiden voyage. Hays accepted but, ever the businessman, he insisted that his en-

tourage pay ninety-three pounds, ten shillings, to cover incidental expenses. Travelling first class with Hays and his wife were their daughter and her husband, their maid and Hays's personal male secretary.

An hour before *Titanic* hit the iceberg, Hays was in the ship's first-class smoking lounge enjoying a drink and a cigar with several other gentlemen. One of these was Col. Archibald Gracie, who survived the disaster. He later wrote that the discussion at the table centred on technological advancements in (then) modern transportation and, at one point, Hays had noted that despite *Titanic* being "a superlative vessel," he was concerned that "the trend to playing fast and loose with larger and larger ships will end in tragedy."

A prudent man, Hays quickly gathered together the members of his entourage and got them to the sinking *Titanic*'s boat deck. He helped his wife, his daughter and the family maid into Lifeboat Number Three — the fourth lifeboat away.

Hays was confident that *Titanic* would stay afloat for ten hours, he told his wife, and that everyone would be rescued. Being in the lifeboat was just a precaution, he added.

Less than an hour and a half later, the great liner was gone.

Hays drowned, but his body was recovered by the *Minia* on April 26, the same day that the GTP's new flagship hotel, the Chateau Laurier in Ottawa, was supposed to have opened. The body of his son-in-law, Thornton Davidson, was never recovered, nor was the body of his twenty-two-year-old secretary, Vivian Payne.

Charles Hays's coffin was brought back to Montreal aboard his private railway car, *Canada*, which is now on display at the Canadian Railway Museum near Delson, Quebec. His funeral was one of the largest and most imposing in Montreal's history.

He was eulogized as one of this nation's greatest citizens. Dean Peterson of McGill University described Hays as "a great-hearted man...who was a real leader of men [and] a true captain of industry."

The Reverend T. S. McWilliams of Cleveland, Ohio, described Hays as being not merely a national figure but also an international one.

Not long after Hays's death, the Grand Trunk Pacific reneged on its agreement with Ottawa to operate its new transcontinental railroad, and its parent company, the Grand Trunk Railway, was put into receivership in 1919. The federal government, in turn, bought up the railway's de-valued stock. During the proceedings, it was alleged by some of the railway's former board of directors that Hays had deceived them in 1903. They said that they would never have endorsed the pricey plan to build Canada's second national railroad, especially since it led to the insolvency and nationalization of the entire Grand Trunk system.

Ottawa proceeded to purchase another independent railway, the Canadian Northern, combining it with the former Grand Trunk to create the Canadian National Railway (CN), which operates, profitably, today.

Interestingly, CN is the only railway in Canada to still offer regular passenger service across the country — aboard its VIA trains. West of Winnipeg, they run exclusively on the railroad first envisioned, and then created, by Charles Hays.

The White Star Line

The **Blue Jacket**, *a 1,790-ton clipper ship, was built in East Boston by Robert E. Jackson and was launched in August 1854, for the White Star Line. It was 235 feet long and had a beam of 41 feet. Her steel hull was painted a dark blue and she carried the carved figure of a sailor, a "blue jacket," on her bow. She sailed from Liverpool on her first voyage to Melbourne, Australia, on March 6, 1855. The trip took sixty-eight days.*

The White Star Line was founded in 1845 by John Pilkington and Henry Wilson, two British entrepreneurs from Liverpool who hoped to cash in on the Australian gold rush of the mid–nineteenth century. Their plan was simple enough: the newly formed shipping line would at first lease and charter vessels instead of purchasing them outright. Then, as their business increased and its capital became established, the fledging company would purchase vessels of its own.

The White Star's first ship was the 879-ton barque *Iowa*, purchased in 1853. In just one month that year,

32,000 would-be gold prospectors departed from Liverpool for Australia. In three years, the colony's population increased by more than one million persons.

But competition for Australia-bound passengers and freight was stiff. A wooden sailing ship of the day, like the *Iowa*, typically took ten weeks to make the trip. Faster, iron-hulled steam ships were seen as the answer.

After several failed mergers with other shipping companies, White Star acquired its first steamship, the *Royal Standard*, in 1863. Instead of the long and dangerous route to Australia, though, the company chose

First-class dining salon aboard the **Baltic**

Liverpool to New York for its new route. North America was now the destination of choice for Europe's emigrants. The shipping line was banking on it!

However, the *Royal Standard* had several flaws. Most notably, she was under-powered. Her top speed was six to eight knots, which was slower than the fastest clipper ships. White Star struggled financially as a result, losing much-needed customers. As a result, the line's directors started mortgaging the company's hard assets, including the *Royal Standard*. Most of these debts were assumed by the Royal Bank of Liverpool.

In 1867 the bank revealed that the White Star Line, now facing bankruptcy, owed it more than half a million pounds. The following year, on January 18, 1868,

Thomas Ismay, then a director of the National Line, purchased the White Star's house flag, trade name and goodwill from the Royal Bank for one thousand pounds.

The thirty year-old Ismay had a knack for making money with ships. He sold off the White Star's wooden-hulled clipper ships, which were still sailing to India and Australia, and he went back to the company's original practice of leasing and chartering vessels, instead of owning them — at least until the shipping line had built up its capital again.

Ismay also entered into an agreement with a prominent Liverpool businessman, Gustav Schwabe, who offered to finance a new line of ships for the White Star

R.M.S. Baltic at Landing Stage, Liverpool
Gross Tonnage 23,876. Extreme Length 725 ft. 9 in. Breadth 75.6.

Baltic *dockside*

Line on the condition that Ismay agree to buy them from his nephew, shipbuilder Gustav Wilhelm Wolff. Wolff was co-owner of the venerable shipyard of Harland and Wolff in Belfast, Ireland.

OCEANIC CLASS

Ismay agreed to buy the ships, but only if Harland and Wolff refused to build other ships for White Star's competitors, such as Cunard. Wolff agreed and work soon commenced on ships of the Oceanic class: the *Atlantic, Baltic* and *Republic*, followed by the slightly larger *Celtic* and *Adriatic*.

In 1871, the White Star Line was back in business on the North Atlantic run, operating between Liverpool and New York, with a stop in Queenstown, Ireland. (Today, the port city is named Cobb.)

The sinking of the *Atlantic* in 1873 near Halifax, Nova Scotia, with a loss of 535 lives, was a major setback for White Star, but the company persevered.

In the last half of the nineteenth century the White Star Line operated many famous liners, such as the *Britannic I*, *Germanic*, *Teutonic* and *Majestic I*. In 1899 Thomas Ismay commissioned one of the most beautiful steamships ever built, the *Oceanic II*. It was the largest ocean liner of its day. From then on, the White Star Line would concentrate on comfort and economy of operation instead of speed.

In 1895, Joseph Bruce Ismay, the son of Thomas

Girls playing aboard the Mauritania

Ismay, took over the position of managing director for the White Star Line. Gustav Wolff had also recently retired, and been replaced by Lord W. J. Pirrie.

In the early twentieth century, a vicious price war developed between the White Star Line and some of its American competitors. International Mercantile Marine Lines (IMM), an aggressive group of Yankees, was, in turn, bought up by the legendary American financier J. P. Morgan. He had started out a railroad man and gone on to make his fortune in coal and steel.

The Cunard Line, White Star's British rival, wasn't standing still. It aimed to stay out in front of all its competitors with two big new ocean liners of its own, *Lusitania* and *Mauritania*.

The writing was on the wall for Ismay and Pirrie. White Star could only remain competitive against Cunard if their shipping line joined Morgan's. By the end of 1902 the deal was final. J. Bruce Ismay would remain White Star's managing director and chairman. At Morgan's insistence, he would later become the president of IMM. Pirrie stayed at the helm of Harland and Wolff.

Ismay was convinced that White Star's future success depended on its ships being big, luxurious and efficient. If they were also fast, so much the better. Likewise, he and J. P. Morgan understood the value in courting Europe's new emigrant class. They both envisioned a new kind of ocean liner that offered "third-

White Star poster

class" accommodations instead of steerage.

In the mid- to late 1800s, "steerage" accommodations below deck had been just that. Eastbound to America, a ship would carry passengers. On the westward return voyage the same ship would carry cattle, usually steers.

The White Star Line had already developed a reputation for comfort. Its Oceanic class of ships had their first-class accommodations located amidship (at the ship's centre), unlike most of its competitors, which had their first-class cabins at the ship's stern, where it was rougher and noiser (from the ship's engines below deck). A grand dining room had also been added and a new feature, the "promenade deck," had been introduced. All Oceanic-class cabins also had running water and electricity.

THE "BIG FOUR"

Between 1901 and 1907, White Star brought into service its "Big Four:" *Celtic*, *Cedric*, *Baltic* and *Adriatic*. Each had a gross displacement of around 24,000 tons (22,000 metric tonnes) and catered mostly to European emigrants, most notably Scandinavians, heading to America. Each ship could accommodate 400 first- and second-class passengers and 2,000 passengers in the new third class. The ships also had huge cargo holds, with each ship capable of carrying up to 17,000 tons (15,500 metric tonnes) of general cargo.

The sinking of the SS Atlantic

Each of the White Star's Big Four ships had better third-class accommodations and service than Cunard ships or other passenger liners of the day, such as those ships of the German Hamburg-American line. This included such niceties as linen tablecloths and silverware in the dining rooms. The menu cards doubled as White Star postcards, which third-class diners could use to write their relatives back home about what a fantastic time they were having aboard ship.

In 1907, Ismay and Pirrie decided on building the biggest and best class of ocean liner ever. The class, and the first ship, would be named Gigantic. It would be the last word in luxury and each ship of the class would be around 1,000 feet (300 metres) long.

But the class's name was changed to Olympic — it was felt that "Gigantic" was too much. Three ships were planned: *Olympic*, *Titanic* and *Britannic II*. (The name Gigantic was also dropped for an individual ship.) The *Olympic* was the only one of the three ships to be a success. It served throughout World War I and into the 1930s, earning the nickname "Old Reliable." It was scrapped in 1937.

The *Titanic* sank in 1912 and the *Britannic II*, which was requisitioned as a hospital ship by the British government during WWI, also went to the bottom after hitting a German mine in the Aegean on November 21, 1916.

Despite the loss of those ships and many others during WWI, the White Star Line went on to become one of the most successful shipping lines of the time.

The Olympic *in Halifax*

What spelled the end for White Star, and all passenger liners in general, was the advent of commercial passenger aviation in the 1930s.

In 1927, controlling interest in the company was returned to British interests. J. P. Morgan could see what was ahead. He knew that it was only a matter of time before the airplane would become the preferred mode of passenger transportation. IMM sold its holdings in White Star to the British-owned Royal Mail Steam Packet Company (Royal Mail Group).

A scandal erupted in 1931 when it became clear that the chairman of the Royal Mail Group, Lord Kyl-sant (Owen Philips), had been "cooking the books," overstating the company's annual financial returns. The "Lord of the Seven Seas," as he was then called, was arrested and charged with corporate fraud. After a nine-day trial, he was sentenced to one year in prison.

Meanwhile, with its financial problems exposed, the Royal Mail Group declared bankruptcy. It, in turn, was bought up by Royal Mail Lines in 1932.

The Great Depression of the 1930s financially crippled the White Star Line and most other shipping lines. In 1933, the British government offered a bailout package to both it and Cunard, but only on the condition

Turkish steam bath on the **Olympic**

that the two great shipping lines merged. By the end of that year, the deal was done.

In 1934 the newly consolidated company would operate as the Cunard White Star Line. White Star contributed ten ships to the new company, while Cunard added fifteen ships. Over the next decade and a half Cunard would continue to buy up White Star stock until 1949, when it owned the company outright. It then reverted to using only the house name Cunard.

The French passenger tender *Nomadic*, the last surviving vessel of the White Star Line, was purchased by the government of Northern Ireland in 2006. She has since been returned to Belfast and is being restored under the auspices of the Nomadic Preservation Trust with the co-operation of her original builders, Harland and Wolff.

The Cunard Line itself was bought out in 1998 by the Carnival Corporation, based in Florida. In addition, it owns Princess Cruises, the Holland America Line and almost a dozen more, making it the largest shipping line in the world. In 2005, Cunard's assets were transferred to Carnival's Princess Cruises division in California. The shipping line is now managed from there.

The *Queen Mary II*, launched in 2003, was the largest passenger liner in the world until 2010. As a tribute to the White Star Line, Cunard introduced its "White Star Service" as the name of the brand of services offered aboard ship. The company has also created the "White Star Academy," an in-house training programme to prepare new crew members for Cunard ships.

BESS ALLISON
Tragedy Personified

Bessie (Bess) Daniels was born in Milwaukee, Wisconsin, on November 14, 1886. She was the youngest daughter of Arville and Sarah Daniels. Her father was a clerk at a meat packing plant.

She met her future husband, Hudson (Hud) Allison, on a train. He was a bookish young man, only five years older than she was. He was later described as "exemplifying the Protestant work ethic." For Bess, he was a dream.

Her new husband was an up-and-coming stockbroker in Montreal. He had joined his uncle, George Johnston, in his bond and investment brokerage firm, Johnston, McConnell and Allison. The other of the trio was John Wilson McConnell, who would go on to own the *Montreal Star* newspaper.

As his uncle's protegé, Hud Allison had spent two years in Winnipeg, where he opened an insurance office selling Sun and New York Life policies.

While there, he got to know Winnipeggers Mark Fortune and Thomson Beattie.

Prior to his joining the Montreal firm, his uncle had sent him to Buffalo, New York, to learn shorthand. It was while he was there that he met Bess.

They were married later that year, 1907, after Bess turned twenty-one years old, and settled into a new home in Montreal's fashionable Westmount district. Two years later, in 1909, their first child, Helen Lorraine, was born.

Hud's investment business was rapidly expanding. He routinely travelled to Europe, and often took Bess with him. In February 1910, Bess's mother, Sarah, joined Hud, her daughter (then eight months pregnant) and one-year-old Lorraine on a trip to England, accompanied by Hud's uncle George and his family. They travelled aboard another famous ocean liner of the day, the *Empress*

Allison farmhouse
Left: Hudson Allison

of Ireland, which sank four years later, at the end of May 1914, in the St. Lawrence River near Rimouski, Quebec. More paying passengers died in that disaster than in the sinking of *Titanic*.

On May 7, 1911, the Allison's second child, Trevor, was born.

By then Hud was a multi-millionaire. In addition to making money, his other passion was farming. He had grown up on a farm near Chesterville, Ontario. He bought it from his father and kept an impressive stable of horses and prize-winning Holstein cows there. He spent as much time at the farm as he could, dividing his time between it and working in Montreal.

Hud Allison was on the board of directors for the British Canadian Lumber Corporation and planned to attend its annual general meeting in London in the spring of 1912. He thought the trip would be a good family outing for Bess and the children.

It would also be a gala shopping trip. He intended to buy some new livestock for the farm and Bess wanted to acquire some new furnishings for both of their homes — the farmhouse in Ontario and the mansion in Montreal. The couple was also looking to employ a staff: a cook, a chauffeur, a maid for Bess and a nurse for baby Trevor.

On that trip the Allisons travelled to England with family friends, John and Emma Thompson McBride and their family, who returned to Canada in February. The Allisons stayed on until April so

Death by the Numbers

Bodies arriving at the Mayfair Curling Club in Halifax, which had been turned into a temporary morgue

On Tuesday, April 16, the cable ship *Mackay-Bennett* from Halifax was hired by the White Star Line, at the rate of $550 per day, to recover the *Titanic's* victims. It headed to sea the next day with several undertakers aboard, 125 coffins lashed to its main deck, and 100 tons of ice in its forward hold.

They headed to the last known co-ordinates of the late great liner. Five days later, sixty-two miles away, they found a pack of 190 bodies intertwined together. With the exception of one little girl's body, they were all wearing lifebelts.

Captain Frederick Lardner later described the bodies as looking, from a distance, like a flock of seagulls on the water: "All we could see at first was the tops of the life preservers. They (the victims) were all floating face upwards, apparently standing in the water."

Lardner later said that most appeared to have died from hypothermia. He recorded the sea's temperature at twenty-eight degrees Fahrenheit (minus two degrees Celsius).

It was apparent to all aboard the *Mackay-Bennett* that another ship was going to be needed to handle the great number of bodies. The Western Union's cable ship, *Minia,* was chartered on Monday, April 22, and headed to sea.

The day before, the crew of the *Mackay-Bennett* had recovered fifty-one bodies, and twenty-six more were recovered on Monday.

The ship's cutters, manned by five crewmen each, would pluck the bodies from the sea, transferring them onto the *Mackay-Bennett*. The ship, in turn, directed the men in the tiny boats towards bodies in the water by tooting its steam whistle. Lookouts were posted from the ship's bridge to its forecastle.

Because there were so many dead, the decision was made by Captain Lardner to bury some of the bodies at sea. Those who could not be identified from their personal effects were committed to the deep.

Twenty-four were sent to Davy Jones's Locker on Sunday and fifteen more on Monday.

By Tuesday, April 23, supplies such as canvas and embalming fluid were running low. Late in the day, the *Mackay-Bennett* was able to meet up with the ocean liner *Sardinian*, which transferred over all the spare canvas it had.

The next day, Wednesday, April 24, another seventy-seven *Titanic* victims were buried at sea. In total, 116 dead were committed to the deep for eternity.

On Thursday, April 25, the *Mackay-Bennett* picked up another eighty-seven bodies. The *Minia* arrived on scene the next day, and both ships spent the morning combing the sea for more bodies.

By noon, the crew of the *Mackay-Bennett* had picked up another fourteen. After that, it headed for Halifax. In total, the ship had recovered 306 individuals, returning to port on April 30 with 190 bodies. It was dubbed "the Death Ship" by reporters waiting onshore.

On Friday, April 26, the crew of the *Minia* found eleven bodies. After that, they only came upon a few more of *Titanic's* dead before heading for home on Friday, May 3. In total, the ship found seventeen bodies, two of which they buried at sea.

The ship's doctor, Dr. William Mosher, described the scene in a letter he later sent his sister: "The weather had turned foggy and the sea rough. By then, the bodies had scattered. The *Minia* picked up some as far away as 150 nautical miles northeast of where *Titanic* sank."

Their "star corpse" was that of Charles Hays, president of the Grand Trunk Railway.

Two more ships were sent out to search for *Titanic* victims, although it was clear by then that the chances of finding any more were slim to none. The Canadian government cutter *Montmagny* made two trips in May; it found one body on Thursday, May 9, and three more the next day.

The last body recovered belonged to twenty-seven-

Concerned relatives on both sides of the Atlantic checking for the names of loved ones

year-old James McGrady. He had been a first-class steward aboard *Titanic*. His body was recovered on May 22 by the *Algerine* from St. John's. On June 6, it was shipped to Halifax aboard another vessel.

McGrady (Body No. 330) was buried at the Fairview Lawn Cemetery in Halifax on June 11, 1912, along with those *Titanic* victims whose bodies couldn't be identified or who weren't claimed by relatives.

In total, 1,502 individuals died in the *Titanic* disaster. Overall, seventy per cent of those on board perished. Of these, only twenty-two per cent were recovered. The bodies of the other seventy-eight per cent were never found.

Members of the ship's crew fared the worst — seventy-six per cent of them died. Third-class passengers were nearly as unlucky; seventy-five per cent of them perished. Sixty per cent of *Titanic's* second-class passengers also died.

Only forty per cent of its first-class passengers were killed.

Seven hundred and five individuals survived.

Hudson Allison with horse and carriage

that Hud could attend his meeting.

Beforehand, they travelled to Banks, Scotland, where Hud bought several teams of Clydesdale horses from a breeder.

In London, the couple rented a house. There, they interviewed many applicants for the different staff positions. They hired eighteen-year-old Mildred Brown as a cook, twenty-six-year-old George Swane as chauffeur, thirty-three-year-old Sarah Daniels as a maid and twenty-two-year-old Alice Cleaver as a nursemaid.

Over the years since the *Titanic* disaster, there's been much speculation as to who, exactly, Alice Cleaver was. Some allege that she was the notorious baby-killer Alice Mary Cleaver, who was con-

victed in 1909 of murdering the infant she bore out of wedlock. Others say that she was Alice Catherine Cleaver, the daughter of a London postman.

Some sources, post-sinking, described her as "a competent nursemaid" and "a thoroughly respectable wife and mother." For this to be true, she would likely have been much older than her alleged twenty-two years of age.

It has been suggested that the Allisons, in fact, knew that she was a convicted murderer — that, being devout Methodists, they took pity on her and gave her a second chance and a new start.

What is known is that upon reaching New York aboard *Carpathia*, the Allison's nursemaid lied to authorities when she was asked her name. She told

On the deck of the Titanic

them that it was "Jean," not Alice, Cleaver.

Though most other *Titanic* survivors were talking, she never gave an interview to any reporter.

What became of Alice Cleaver after the disaster is also a mystery. Some allege that she returned to England, married, and died in 1984. If so, she would have been ninety-five years old at the time of her death, making her one of the longest-living *Titanic* survivors. That's if she was only twenty-two years old at the time of the disaster.

Others have said that she didn't, in fact, return to England. Instead, she changed her name and stayed in the United States, dying in Ohio.

The Allison entourage boarded the *Titanic* at Southampton. Hud and Bess Allison occupied one cabin in their first-class parlour suite while the newly hired maid, Sarah Daniels, slept in the same cabin with their daughter Lorraine and the new nursemaid, Alice Cleaver, slept in the same cabin as baby Trevor.

Chauffeur George Swane and cook Mildred Brown travelled in separate second-class cabins.

That last fateful night, Sunday, April 14, Bess and Hud Allison dined with Arthur Peuchen, from Toronto, and Harry Molson, from Montreal, in the *Titanic's* first-class dining room. Partway through dinner the maid, Sarah Daniels, brought little Lorraine Allison down to visit her parents and to see the grand room. One can imagine the men at the table fussing good-naturedly over the little girl.

Above: A trunk recovered at the surface days after Titanic *had foundered*
Above left: Blouse found inside a trunk found on the surface
Left: Pocket watch recovered from a victim found floating on the surface after Titanic *sunk*

What happened to most of the Allison family after that is debatable. One version of events has it that Alice Cleaver hurriedly dressed baby Trevor and headed for the boat deck after she learned of the collision with the iceberg. Apparently, she did so without telling either of the Allisons in the room next door. Once topside, she climbed aboard Lifeboat Number 11 when the call came, "Women and children only, please."

While on the *Carpathia*, Mildred Brown wrote a letter to her mother back in England. In it, she wrote, "No sooner was I on deck that I was pushed into one of the boats and I found nurse (Alice Cleaver) and the baby (Trevor Allison) were there."

Arthur Peuchen, who had dined with the couple only hours before, later told the Montreal *Daily Star* that Bess Allison was frantic to find her baby boy. She had become separated from her husband, who was likely also searching for baby Trevor and Alice Cleaver. This seems to confirm that Alice

Cleaver hadn't said anything to the Allisons about taking their child with her.

At one point, Bess and Lorraine Allison were put aboard a lifeboat by an officer (likely Lifeboat Number 8), Peuchen said, but Bess Allison wouldn't leave her husband and son behind and climbed out of the lifeboat, dragging two-year-old Lorraine behind her.

"Mrs. Allison could have gotten away in perfect safety. But someone told her that Mr. Allison was in a boat being lowered on the opposite side of the ship. With her little daughter, she rushed away from the boat. Apparently, she reached the other side to find that Mr. Allison was not there. Meanwhile, our boat had put off," Peuchen told the reporter from the *Star*.

Whether she found her husband before the end isn't known, nor will it ever be known if they learned what happened to their son, Trevor. It's possible that their chauffeur George Swane, who also didn't survive *Titanic*'s sinking, told them that Alice Cleaver and young Trevor were in the same lifeboat as cook Mildred Brown, providing he recognized Cleaver.

Lorraine Allison's nanny, Sarah Daniels, survived, escaping aboard Lifeboat Number 8. Lorraine was the only child in first and second class to die. Her body was not recovered, nor was her mother's; only Hudson's body was found by the *Mackay-Bennett*. He was dressed in a blue suit with a leather coat and a grey silk scarf. He wore a pair of gold cufflinks, a gold lapel stud, a silver tie clip and a diamond solitaire ring. He was buried in his family's plot in the country cemetery near where he grew up.

A month after his funeral, his brother Percy got a telephone call at the Allison farm. The Scottish draught horses bought by his brother had arrived

Lifeboat Number 14 towing Collapsible D to Carpathia

in Chesterville by train, having travelled across the ocean by tramp steamer.

On his arrival in New York, baby Trevor was claimed by his great-uncle George Allison from Montreal. He was raised by Uncle George and Aunt Lillian.

In the summer of 1929, when he was eighteen years old, while visiting his grandparents (Bess's parents) Trevor Allison got sick from eating a spoiled sandwich made from beef's tongue but refused to see a doctor. He took a train to Maine, where his aunt, uncle and cousins were vacationing, and died there on August 7.

His body was sent to Chesterville, Ontario, where he was laid to rest beside his father.

Whose Fault Was It?

THE U.S. SENATE INVESTIGATES

After the *Titanic* disaster, the governments of both the United States and England held their own separate inquiries. The U.S. one was held in Washington, D.C., over eighteen days starting in late April 1912. Eighty-six witnesses were called and over one thousand pages of testimony were entered into the record.

Senator William Smith from Michigan chaired the U.S. Senate's Committee on Commerce, which reviewed the accident. It unanimously put the blame on *Titanic*'s captain, Edward Smith, some of the ship's senior officers, Bruce Ismay, president of the White Star Line, and the shipping line itself.

> *His (Capt. Smith's) indifference to danger was one of the direct and contributing causes of this unnecessary tragedy.*

Despite receiving several warnings from other ships earlier in the day of ice ahead, *Titanic*'s speed was actually increased, when it should have been decreased, Senator Smith noted.

> *...danger seemed to stimulate her (*Titanic*) to action rather than to persuade her to fear.*

Also, he blamed another ship, the *Californian*, for not coming to *Titanic*'s aid. It had stopped for the night just to the north because of the ice field in front of it, only hours before *Titanic* collided with the iceberg.

Despite seeing and signalling *Titanic*, the *Californian*'s crew did nothing to help the sinking liner, even after *Titanic* fired its distress rockets, Senator Smith said,

> *Had he (Stanley Lord, *Californian*'s captain) been (more) vigilant, there is a*

very strong probability that every human life that was sacrificed through this disaster could have been saved.

The disaster could also have been averted, the senator said, if only the ship's second-in-command, Second Officer Charles Lightoller, had forced open the *Titanic*'s binocular box on the bridge so that the lookouts in the crow's nest could use them. Lookout Frederick Fleet testified that he was used to having binoculars. He had used a pair when he served aboard the *Oceanic* before being assigned to *Titanic*, and he had used *Titanic*'s between Southampton and Queenstown, Ireland.

Senator Smith also blamed the White Star Line for not having a safety policy in place aboard *Titanic*.

> *No general alarm was given, no ship's officers formally assembled, no orderly routine was attempted or organized system of safety begun. Haphazard, they rushed by one another on (the) staircase and in (the) hallway!*

Smith pointed out that another 500 lives could have been saved if *Titanic*'s lifeboats had been loaded to capacity.

He also accused some of *Titanic*'s officers of cowardliness. Some never reported to their station and were quick to desert the ship, he said.

> *Some of the men, to whom had been intrusted the care of passengers, never reported to their official stations, and quickly deserted the ship with a recklessness and indifference to the responsibilities of their positions as culpable and amazing as it is impossible to believe.*

But he praised the courage of *Titanic*'s two wireless operators, especially senior operator Jack Philips, who didn't survive: "Their faithfulness is worthy of the highest praise."

Smith praised Captain Arthur Rostron and the crew of the rescue ship *Carpathia*:

With most touching detail he promptly ordered the ship's officers to their stations, distributed the doctors into positions of greatest usefulness, prepared comforts for man and mother and babe; with foresight and tenderness he lifted them from their watery imprisonment and, when the rescue had been completed, summoned all of the rescued together and ordered the ship's bell tolled for the lost, and asked that prayers of thankfulness be offered by those who had been spared. It falls to the lot of few men to perform a service so unselfish, and the American Congress can honor itself no more by any single act than by writing into its laws the gratitude we feel toward this modest and kindly man.

Smith also called for more safety regulations:

Regulation of steamship transportation is as necessary as regulation of railroad transportation....Transportation by rail is conducted through settled localities, where many residents would quickly discover and immediately report any irregularities or disregard of safety requirements, while by water it is conducted beyond the criticism of any except the actual passengers of the ship, making it all the more necessary for definite regulations.

Captain Edward Smith

At the end of the proceedings, the committee moved to amend Bill 6976, which regulated navigation by steam passenger vessels, and it recommended the creation of a government committee to review, and update as needed, the laws and regulations for the construction and outfitting of vessels, especially with radios, navigational aids and lifesaving equipment.

JAKOB ALFRED JOHANSON
Wanderlust Did Him In

Mid-nineteenth century loggers, Portland, Oregon

Jakob Johanson was a man who couldn't sit still. As a boy, he spent most of his time outdoors on his parents's farm near the village of Munsala on the west coast of Finland. Sometimes he would go out in a boat with his father and uncles to fish for cod and herring.

He would often go down to the shore and skip stones out into the Baltic Sea's Gulf of Bothina, called the "Great Eastern Lake" in the time of the Vikings. The young Jakob would stand on the beach and look west across the water towards neighbouring Sweden, imagining himself as a sea-faring adventurer of old.

When he turned nineteen, the wanderlust took hold and he headed to America to seek his fortune. Like so many other Scandinavians of the day, he headed for the great forests of the Pacific Northwest. From then on he went by the first name of "Fred."

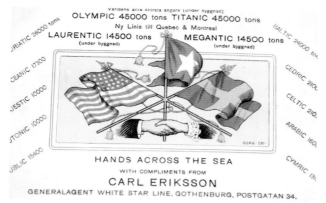

Portland, Oregon, situated near where the Willamette and Columbia rivers meet, must have seemed like heaven — Valhalla — to the young Finn. The "Oregon Territory" had only been discovered by famed explorers Lewis and Clark less than ninety years before. In the 1850s, the area's first water-powered sawmills were up and running. Lumber was shipped overseas by boat to ports as far away as Australia and China. In 1883, the transcontinental railroad arrived, opening up more markets in the eastern U.S.

By the mid-nineteenth century, farming and logging were mainstays of the local economy, and most of this was being done by newly arrived immigrants, mostly from Scandinavia. Working in the Blue Mountains, they cut down giant softwoods, Douglas fir and western red cedar, using only saws and axes. Men with teams of horses would haul the giant logs to the river's edge, where even more men would roll them in to float downriver to the newly constructed Northwest paper mill at Camas.

When Fred Johanson arrived in 1896, Portland was one busy place. Large-scale logging was happening across the entire Columbia River Basin, and would continue until around 1910. The place was raucous and rowdy.

Above: Third-class accomodation
Top left: Calling card

Erickson's WorkingMan's Club

Erikson's Workingman's Club

Hardworking "woodmen" were known to enjoy a pint of beer or two at the end of a long work day. They frequented Portland's many saloons and breweries. In fact, the city had been dubbed "Beervaria," because of the many fine ales available there, brewed up by recently immigrated German beer meisters.

One notable establishment was Erickson's Workingman's Club in the city's north end. It was started by August "Gus" Erickson, a Russian Finn and one-time logger. The joint was monstrously large, occupying almost an entire city block.

Erickson boasted that his saloon was the best in the world. It did have the world's longest bar — 684 feet long! The place had five elegant entrances and a huge grand pipe organ (which cost $5,000 and had been imported from Europe), and employed fifty bartenders.

Erickson's was also the home of the "free lunch," a smorgasbord of sliced sausages, Scandinavian cheeses, pickled herring and hardtack bread, which could all be had for the price of a nickel glass of beer.

So beloved was the place that when the river rose in 1894 and flooded Portland's downtown, serious patrons rowed their boats to a makeshift barge Gus Erickson had constructed so that no one would miss a moment of the Workingman's Club experience.

Portland author and historian Stewart Holbrook immortalized the place in his story "Elbow Bending for Giants." In it, he paints a picture of a classic encounter between the formidable Erickson's bouncer, Jumbo Reilly, and a rowdy Swedish logger, "Halfpint" Halverson:

One of Erikson's girls

On one occasion when Halfpint disregarded Jumbo's warning, the bouncer plucked Halverson by the collar and pants and threw him bodily out the Second Avenue entrance.

Halverson presently wandered in through one of the three Burnside Street doors. Out he went again in a heap. This continued until he had been ejected through four different doors.

Working his way around to the Third Avenue side, Halverson made his entry through the fifth, and last, door. Just inside, stood the mountainous Jumbo. Halverson stopped short.

"Yesus!" said he. "Vas yo bouncer en every goddam saloon en Portland?"

Upstairs, there was a theatre with dancing girls who drummed up business for their other, much more lucrative, line of work "entertaining" the saloon's patrons in small, five-by-six-foot rooms on the floor above. Erickson's girls were said to be the prettiest in all of Portland.

In 1901, twenty-four-year-old Johanson married another Finn immigrant, the beautiful Anna Lovisa Andersson. It's not known where or how they met, but the young couple would have four children, two boys and two girls.

The Klondike

Whether he had tired of toiling day after day in Oregon's forests or he had had a run-in with Erickson's "Jumbo Reilly," Johanson left his family for greener pastures. This time, he headed even further north, to Alaska and the Klondike Gold Rush!

The same year that Johanson arrived in America, 1896, gold had been discovered in Rabbit "Bonanza" Creek. News of the strike quickly travelled south and around the world. By the next summer, would-be fortune hunters and prospectors were heading north from both Portland and Seattle, Washington.

A significant financial recession gripped the U.S. in the 1890s and a number of banks had failed. The American economy had been hard hit by the "Panic of 1893" and the "Panic of 1896," which caused widespread unemployment. As a result, many men who had fallen on hard times were motivated to try their luck panning and digging for gold.

Men from all walks of life, from all over the world, headed for the gold fields of the Yukon. Surprisingly, a large number were former professionals, including teachers and doctors, even a mayor or two! Many gave up respectable careers to make the journey. One resident of "Camp Skagway Number One" was Frederick Russell Burnham, a celebrated American Army scout, who arrived from Africa only to be called back to take part in the Second Boer War.

Most of the would-be gold labourers were perfectly aware that their chances of finding significant amounts of gold were slim to none but they went anyway. Most didn't stay on, though. Some returned home, while others found new lives in Alaska, Western Canada and the Pacific Northwest.

"Stampeders" landed at the Alaskan towns of Skagway and Dyea. From there, they hiked the Chilkoot Trail, crossing the notorious Chilkoot Pass or they trekked up the White Pass to Lake Lindeman, or Bennett Lake, at the headwaters of the Yukon River. From there, they then travelled by rafts or boats down the Yukon River to Dawson City, a distance of some five-hundred-plus miles (eight-hundred-plus kilometres).

Aware of what happened during previous gold strikes in the U.S., in Canada the North West Mounted Police (the forerunners of the modern-day Royal Canadian Mounted Police, the "Mounties") kept a tight lid on things. One of the Mounties' requirements was that each prospector carry with him a one-year's supply of goods, most of which was food. This amounted to approximately a ton of supplies per man, and made purveyors of such goods in ports like Portland, Seattle and Vancouver wealthy men.

The Mounties also weren't having any gunplay like the kind the American "Wild West" had been known for. All firearms, such as rifles and shotguns, had to be accounted for, and no handguns were allowed — period!

The Canadian lawmen had every reason to take such precautions. Overburdened with gear, most of the would-be prospectors ended up either losing or dumping most of their possessions before arriving in Dawson City. As a result, the rapidly expanding city routinely

Working girls of the Klondike

Panning for gold in the Klondike

Miners wait to register a claim

experienced acute shortages of food, medicine and other much-needed goods. The Mounties knew that in desperate times desperate men were prone to take desperate actions, more so if they were heavily armed.

The Mounties also feared prospectors being robbed of their gold by other prospectors, thieves, card sharps and con men, bushwhackers, and gangsters from the notorious Skagway Gang led by Soapy Smith. All were good reasons for the Mounties wanting to control the amount of firearms in the territory.

By the time most of the would-be prospectors arrived in Dawson City, most gold claims had already been staked out. Although the Klondike Gold Rush would last into the 1920s, it reached its height in 1908.

Fred Johanson was one of the Klondike's fortunate ones. As with any commodity, whether it's mining for gold or investing in the stock market, making a profit is about knowing when to get in and when to get out. Johanson got there and back to Oregon before 1907.

The fit young Finn would have had little trouble managing the arduous, and dangerous, trek to Dawson City. Well-accustomed to working year-round in the outdoors, he would have been right at home in the forests of the Yukon River area. He also had the advantage of having lived in the U.S., learning to speak English and acclimatize to the customs and culture there.

Flush with cash, Johanson was able to move his entire family back to Finland, where he bought a farm near his parents. The family settled into a comfortable life, but it wasn't enough for the modern-day Viking.

Period postcard of the Adriatic
Opposite page (top): First-class dining salon on the Adriatic
Opposite page (bottom left): First-class smoking lounge on the Adriatic
Opposite page (bottom right): First-class ladies reading room on the Adriatic

After his experiences in Portland and the Klondike allowed him to return to Finland, Jakob settled down — but only for a while. In 1912 he sold his farm to his brother, Hannes, and bought himself a ticket to make another transatlantic crossing, but this time his destination would be Vancouver, British Columbia. Why, no one can say. Perhaps he planned to return to the Klondike. Perhaps he planned to return to Oregon. All that's known for sure is that he travelled without his family.

Johanson originally booked passage on another White Star ship, the *Adriatic*, but his ticket was transferred to *Titanic* because of an ongoing coal strike in England. Aboard the great liner on its maiden voyage, Johanson fell in with several other Finns from around Munsala — Jakob and Alfred Wiklund, Karl Johan and young Anna Sjoblom. She had gone to school with Jakob Wiklund, and was travelling with the three young men to Olympia, Washington, to meet up with her brother, Daniel, and her father, Gabriel. Both had gone ahead several years before and had made a new life there as woodsmen. In fact,

Above: Second-class library aboard the Adriatic
Left: Third-class dining room aboard the Adriatic

Sunday, April 14, 1912, was Anna's eighteenth birthday. The small group celebrated her birthday together, although Sjoblom wasn't much in the mood for a party. She was prone to seasickness and had been sick most of the trip. This turned out to be a good thing because it helped save her life.

She slept fully dressed in case she had to go to the bathroom. When *Titanic* hit the iceberg, Sjoblom quickly got out of bed and headed topside. Speaking no English, the frightened teenager found her way to the second-class Promenade on A Deck and was able to climb a crew ladder to *Titanic*'s boat deck, where she boarded Lifeboat Number 16. It was lowered away at 1:35 a.m. on

Adriatic *passengers*

Monday, April 15 — less than one hour before *Titanic* foundered. She never saw her travelling companions again; she was the only one of her little group to survive.

Johanson's body was recovered several days later by the *Mackay-Bennett*. He was thirty-four years old at the time of *Titanic*'s sinking. The bodies of the other three men were not found.

On his person were some papers, a comb, a set of keys, a pocket knife, a fountain pen, a locket, a gold watch and chain, a handful of coins in a small purse and $264 in bills. All these were returned to his wife, Anna, in Finland. Anna Johanson remarried in 1917, and died in 1937.

Jakob "Fred" Johanson was buried in Halifax's Fairview Lawn Cemetery.

Sjoblom went on to prove that she was a "survivor" in the true sense of the word. She married twice and lived to the age of eighty-one, dying of a stroke in 1975. She was buried in Tacoma's Mountain View Cemetery.

WILLIAM EDWY RYERSON

A Soldier's Sense of Duty Saved Him

Aformer professional soldier, William Ryerson survived *Titanic*'s sinking because of his sense of duty, though working as a second-class dining room steward aboard the late great liner was a far cry from his days as a fighting man in both the British and Canadian armies.

He was born in 1878 near the small rural community of Port Dover, Ontario, to Catherine and George Arthur Ryerson. His father, a distinguished army captain, had retired to farm on the north shore of Lake Ontario.

William Ryerson longed for the adventurous life of a professional soldier, and signed up with the army when he was eighteen. That same year, 1899, the South African War began. More commonly known as the Boer War, it started after many years of political unrest between the ruling British and South Africa's Dutch settlers, known as the "Boers"

(from the Dutch for "farmer").

A decade before, gold had been discovered in the Transvaal, an independent republic in the northern part of the country. Fortune hunters, mostly from England, flooded into the region, straining relations with the resident Boers. Things came to a head when Britain reinforced its military garrison. On October 9, the Transvaal territorial government issued an ultimatum, demanding that the British cease its build-up. London did not reply, and on October 11, 1899, the Boers declared war.

The British Empire was at its height in 1899. London viewed the Boers as being backwards and incapable of standing up to British might. While it was true that the Boers were outgunned and outnumbered, they were determined. They put up a stiff resistance to British forces.

Canada's prime minister at the time, Sir Wilfrid

Laurier, was reluctant to send troops to South Africa — it would be Canada's first overseas war. He was especially concerned about the opposition to the war in Quebec. French-Canadian nationalist Henri Bourassa led this opposition. He described the war as nothing more than an example of British imperialism and feared that it would lead to even more conflicts in the future.

After considerable pressure from British loyalists in Ontario, Laurier relented. To limit criticism from the likes of Bourassa, the Canadian contingent would be made up of volunteers and professional soldiers; there would be no conscripts.

In December, fierce fighting broke out between the two sides. Until the end of January, 1900, the Boers advanced south into British territory, scoring several important victories. In February, British forces counterattacked, capturing Transvaal's capital, Pretoria. It was there that Canadian soldiers saw action for the first time.

The contingent consisted of the 2nd (Special Service) Battalion from the Royal Canadian Regiment of Infantry. On February 18, 1900, it suffered its first casualties while advancing on Boer positions after crossing the Modder River. Participating in an ill-conceived and unsuccessful charge ordered by the acting British commander, Lord Herbert Kitchener, the Canadian regiment suffered eighteen dead and sixty-three wounded infantrymen.

On February 26, the regiment made a daring nighttime raid, capturing the Boer position at Paardeberg. It was a major victory for the British. The British commander-in-chief for the regiment, Lord Frederick Roberts, said, "'Canadian' now stands for bravery, dash and courage."

Meanwhile, back home, the Laurier government agreed to send a second contingent of Canadians

1st Battalion Canadian Mounted Rifles

to South Africa, but this time it would be made up of mounted troops. The British realized that troopers on horseback would have a huge advantage over foot soldiers. In raising the new mounted unit, the Canadian government searched for men who were already experienced horsemen and good shots.

The unit was originally named the 1st Battalion, Canadian Mounted Rifles, and comprised a total of nineteen officers and 371 men and their horses, organized into two squadrons. The core of each squadron was provided by experienced regulars from the Royal Canadian Dragoons, the cavalry unit of the Canadian Permanent Force. The Dragoons had gained notoriety during the Northwest Rebellion in 1885. Also, a detachment had served in the Yukon Field Force in 1896.

The remainder of the battalion were volunteers from Manitoba and Ontario. Many were members of cavalry regiments of the part-time militia. One of these was young William Ryerson.

The Dragoons, as the unit came to be known, arrived in South Africa at the end of March, 1900. As author John Boileau noted in his recent book *Canada's Soldiers in South Africa*, their arrival caused quite a stir!

> *The appearance of the mounted troops caused great excitement in Cape Town. To the townsfolk, these big, brawny Canadians riding their huge horses on high-horned heavy western stock saddles were something out of the fabled Wild West, with their cowboy hats, high boots, spurs and Colt revolvers. The mounted Canadians were a tough, hard-riding lot and some of their exploits quickly became the stuff of legend.*

One such event happened on November 6 and 7, 1900. A small group of Dragoons were guarding a position near Leliefontein when they were overrun by Boers. The Canadians fought desperately and were able to hold out. In the fighting, two Boer commanders were killed. Three Dragoons, two lieutenants and a sergeant were awarded the Victoria Cross for their bravery. The only other time Canadians earned as many medals in a single action was at Vimy Ridge during World War I.

In total, 7,368 Canadians served in South Africa. Of these, 89 were killed in action and 252 were wounded. Another 138 died of disease. The Royal Canadian Dragoons have been described as being the most effective unit to serve in South Africa.

Once back in Canada, trooper William Ryerson didn't have long to wait until he returned to the battlefield. His next foray would take him even farther afield, fighting in India with a British calvary unit.

At the beginning of the nineteenth century, both the British and Russian Empires struggled for control of what was then India's North-West Frontier. Today, it's known as Afghanistan's Tribal Areas. Several major military conflicts, dubbed the "Great Game" but better known as the "Anglo-Afghan Wars," defined the century in Afghanistan.

The first began in 1838 when Britain invaded. London was fearful of an alliance between its ruler, Dost Mohammed, and Russia's czar, Alexander II. Britain viewed India as the jewel in the crown of the British Empire, and it didn't welcome a Russian presence at its doorstep.

The First Anglo-Afghan War was a complete disaster for the British. By its end, four years later, Britain's entire contingent of 4,500 soldiers (along with 12,000 civilians) had been killed. Most of them had been massacred during the retreat from Kabul through the Khyber Pass. Only one man survived, an army doctor who was sent back to India by Pashtun (Afghan) tribesmen in order to tell London what had happened.

The Second Anglo-Afghan War occurred in 1876, and the Third Anglo-Afghan War was fought in 1919. The periods in between were marked by rebellions with Pashtuns who were determined to claim their independence from British occupation.

After reaching a virtual stalemate in the first

Boer commandos

two wars, the British imposed the "Durand Line" in 1893, which divided Afghanistan and British India's North-West Frontier. For the next twenty-five-odd years, British forces would patrol and defend the artificial border, which it saw as a buffer zone to inhibit the spread of Russian influence into British India. Afghans deeply resented it.

No doubt, William Ryerson would have known about the Pathan Revolt of 1897. During the summer of that year several major battles occurred, including the Siege of Malakand. There, the small British garrison, comprised mostly of two calvary regiments — one British and one Indian — held off an invading Pashtun force of more than 10,000 warriors.

A young second lieutenant with the 4th Hussars and war correspondent, Winston Churchill, described the fight in great detail for the *London Daily Telegraph* in 1898. The story of the Malakand Field Force attracted worldwide attention and launched his career as a public figure. The Siege of Malakand was Churchill's first experience of actual combat.

"Every influence, every motive, that provokes the spirit of murder among men, impels these mountaineers to deeds of treachery and violence," Churchill wrote of the Afghans.

Troopers like Ryerson would have spent their days patrolling valleys such as Peshawar, Kohat, Kurram and Swat, and their nights guarding

British forts at Malakand, Chakadara and other places. They would have related to the words written by Churchill only a few years before: "It was a difficult and unknown country with an enemy who gave the troops no rest and pressed close on the heels of every retirement, while cleverly avoiding resistance in strength to an advance."

The North-West Frontier became a province of India in 1901 under the control of a chief commissioner appointed by London. In 1931, Sir Ralph Griffith was appointed its first governor. The first provincial elections were held in 1937. After India gained its independence from Britain in 1947, the North-West Frontier Province voted in a referendum to join Pakistan. In 1969, Pakistan added several districts and renamed the larger region the "Tribal Areas."

At age twenty-nine, in 1907, William Ryerson married Florence Ann Mallison at Aston, Birmingham County, England. That same year, the couple's first child, Clarence, was born. All told, the Ryersons would have six children.

In 1912, with three young children, thirty-two-year-old William Ryerson was struggling to make ends meet. Since being discharged from the army he had settled in Southamptom, which had been dubbed "the Gateway to the Empire." It was there that he decided to sign on as a second-class dining room steward aboard *Titanic*.

One of his duties as a member of the ship's crew was to man a lifeboat, if the need arose. Most of his colleagues didn't take this responsibility seriously though because, after all, the *Titanic* was considered unsinkable.

But, ever the military man, Ryerson did. His commitment to duty saved his life when he was instructed by First Officer William Murdoch to help out aboard Lifeboat Number 9.

Four out of five of *Titanic's* crew were from Southampton. About one third of all those who perished in the disaster were from the city.

Southampton was also the home port for the transatlantic passenger liners operated by Cunard. After *Titanic*, Ryerson was able to find a position with the line and worked aboard several different ships until the outbreak of World War I in 1914.

Once again, Ryerson was back in uniform. But, this time he fought with the 159th Gun Brigade of the Royal Field Artillery. He served in France and was promoted to the rank of sergeant.

In 1920, he returned to Canada. But, he was no gentleman farmer like his retired army-officer father had been!

He worked at the Firestone Tire & Rubber Co. manufacturing plant in Hamilton, Ontario, for several years. Later, he became a customs officer for the department of National Revenue, Customs and Excise.

In 1937, he chose to return to England with his wife, Florence. He spent the rest of his days there living off his army pension. He died in 1949 at the age of seventy-one.

The "Other" Ryerson

Arthur Ryerson was described by the Chicago *Evening Post*, in his obituary of Tuesday, May 28, 1912, as being a capitalist and steel magnate from Philadelphia and formerly of Chicago. His father had been Joseph Turner Ryerson, founder of Ryerson & Company Iron and Steel Merchants. He had arrived in America in 1842 and had worked as an agent for a Pennsylvania ironmaster, leasing a two-storey building on the banks of the Chicago River.

American industrialization during the last half of the nineteenth century demanded lots of steel for building things such as railroads, railway locomotives and passenger and freight cars. Ryerson & Company quickly became one of the largest processors and distributors of metals in North America, and it remains so today.

In 1996, the company went public. Today, it trades on the New York Stock Exchange under the symbol "RT," which stands for Ryerson Tull. It operates service centres in cities across the U.S. and Canada, and serves an expanding international customer base in China through its subsidiary, Ryerson China Limited.

Arthur Ryerson, age sixty-one, and his wife, Emily, had been in Europe on holiday with two of their three daughters, Emily and Suzette, and their youngest son, Jack, when they learned of the death of their oldest child, Arthur Junior, age twenty. He had been killed in an automobile accident while driving with a friend on Easter Monday. His funeral was to be held on Friday afternoon, April 19, at St. Mark's Episcopal Church in the affluent Philadelphia borough of Haverford.

As a result, the Ryersons cut short their holiday and booked passage on the first homebound ship available, *Titanic*, which was scheduled to reach New York on Wednesday, April 17.

At the time of the collision with the iceberg on Sunday night, April 14, the family was asleep in their first-class staterooms. Emily Ryerson later said that she heard "the horrible grating crash." She and her two daughters threw on kimonos over their nightgowns and rushed barefoot to *Titanic*'s boat deck, she was later quoted as saying.

Together with her three children, she climbed aboard Lifeboat Number 4, on the port side. It was the last regular lifeboat to leave *Titanic*, at 1:55 a.m. After it, only three "collapsible" canvas lifeboats were lowered away. Less than half an hour later, at approximately 2:20 a.m., *Titanic* sank.

In fact, the Ryersons' lifeboat was the closest one to the liner when it foundered. Seven swimmers made it to the boat and were pulled in, but two of them later died of exposure.

Arthur Ryerson stayed aboard the doomed liner, giving his place in a lifeboat to his wife's maid. His body was never recovered.

He was a distant fourth cousin (technically a third cousin once removed) to one of *Titanic*'s "victualing" crew members, William Ryerson (who did survive). Neither man was likely aware of the other's existence.

Arthur Ryerson

BERTHE DE VILLIERS

The Showgirl and the Hockey Player

In her later years, the family of Berthe de Villiers didn't believe her when she said she had been aboard *Titanic*. It was only after her death in 1962, when they found under her bed a shoebox full of old newspaper clippings and mementos, that they finally knew the truth.

Little is known about her earliest days, but by the time she was twenty-four, when she boarded *Titanic*, she was already a cabaret performer of some note and a "woman with a past."

In actual fact, she was born Bertha Antoine Mayne on July 21, 1887, in the small rural, town of Ixelles, Belgium.

She changed her name early on because she thought that "Bertha" conjured up images of pastoral farm life. The great Impressionist painter, Edouard Manet had painted his muse, Berthe Morisot, in 1872, and this name sounded much more sophisticated to young Bertha, who was determined to make her mark on Brussels high society.

Her surname was also her own invention. It too was a deliberate attempt on her part to conceal her working-class roots. She likely took the name from a Belgian nobleman, the Count de Villiers, whose estate was near where she grew up.

Armed with her new persona, she quickly made a name for herself in the cabaret nightclubs of Brussels, Luxemburg and Paris. However, it was not as a performer that she gained notoriety.

Instead, she was better known for the company she kept. The Belgian newspaper *Het Laatste Nieuws* described her as "being well known in circles of pleasure and she is often seen in the company of people who like to wine and dine and enjoy life."

She was said to have been involved with a French

The City of the Night

Called the "city of light," Paris could just as easily have been called the "city of the night" — especially at the turn of the twentieth century. Its famed "Montmartre" nightclub district grew out of the city's bars and brothel district near the Saint Pierre de Montmartre church.

Since the area was outside the Paris city limits, Montmartre was tax exempt. As a result, it became a popular drinking spot towards the end of the nineteenth century. The area was also known for its artist residents and their Bohemian ways. Many of the great Expressionist painters like Claude Monet, Pablo Picasso and Vincent van Gogh lived and worked there.

The Moulin Rouge (the "Red Mill" in French) cabaret was built in 1899 on the Boulevard de Clichy. Then, as now, it was recognizable by the red windmill on its roof. It's best known as the birthplace of the "cancan," which, itself, is credited with being the origin of the modern striptease.

The dance style started out as a respectable working-class party dance, but it evolved into fast-paced seductive exhibitionism on the part of the female partner. Most dancers were prostitutes who used it to entice customers. At first, the dance was performed individually on stage, but later it was performed in a chorus line. The dancers would lift their skirts and reveal their legs. Sometimes they wore lingerie underneath, sometimes they did not!

The growing popularity of music halls in Europe made former high-class brothels, like the Moulin Rouge, acceptable — even fashionable. Other famous nightclubs sprang up, like the Folies Bergere, the Paradis Latin and La Nouvelle Eve.

What had been simply vulgar and overtly sexual became athletic and acrobatic. Performers wore less and less on stage, much to the delight of a mostly male audience. In 1907, an actress by the name of Germaine Aymos performed wearing only three small sea shells, almost bringing the house down from the thunderous applause of patrons.

Cabaret performers came from all walks of life and backgrounds. Many were failed ballet dancers, some were musicians and singers, others had been stage actresses. Some had no formal training at all.

A cabaret performer of the time

World's First Diva

Jeanne Bourgeois, as Mistinguett, was one of the most famous. She started out as a poor flower girl on the street, singing ballads to attract customers. She made her debut in Paris at the Casino du Paris in 1895 and also appeared regularly at the Folies Bergere, the Moulin Rouge and the Eldorado Club. Her risqué routines captivated audiences and she became the highest-paid entertainer of her time.

In 1919 her legs were insured for the then astounding amount of 500,000 francs. She was said to have had the most beautiful legs in the world.

She had a long-time love affair with French actor Maurice Chevalier, who was several years her junior.

She also became a singer, recording her signature song "Mon Homme" in 1916. The English version, "My Man," was popularized by American pop singer Fanny Brice.

At the height of her career, one of her performance dresses could weigh as much as twenty pounds, sometimes dragging a five-yard train. The price tag per outfit, in today's money, was approximately $40,000. It wasn't uncommon for her to wear eleven completely different outfits per cabaret show, including giant sprays of feathers on her head.

She was described as an acrobatic dancer who had a flair for style, décor and production.

As beautiful as Mistinguett was, her contemporary Colette was notorious.

(regular) army officer who had run off to join the French Foreign Legion for reasons unknown. One rumour had it that he had shot a man in a duel over Berthe. Another had it that he went on the lam from the law after committing a robbery, the proceeds of which he spent on his showgirl sweetie.

Around Christmastime in 1911, she met a dashing, and rich, young playboy from Montreal, Quigg Baxter. He first laid eyes on her in the nightclub where she performed, and was instantly smitten.

Theirs was a whirlwind romance. Baxter promised to marry her if she agreed to come back to Canada with him. She did.

His story was equally dark and hedonistic. He was the son of the infamous businessman "Diamond Jim" Baxter. Originally a jeweller from Ontario, the older Baxter first went into loan sharking when he arrived in Montreal. Later, he turned to the stock market, becoming a broker. He amassed a large fortune, with huge real estate holdings.

The Baxter family home stood at the centre of what was known as "the Golden Square Mile," the borough of Montreal's rich and famous. At the beginning of the twentieth century, it was said that seventy per cent of Canada's wealth resided in the neighbourhood.

Their next-door neighbour was William Cornelius Van Horne, president of the Canadian Pacific Railroad. Nearby was the stately mansion of Charles Hays, CEO of the rival Grand Trunk Pacific Railroad.

In 1900, James "Diamond Jim" Baxter was convicted of bank fraud, the result of an elaborate Ponzi scheme, and was sentenced to five years in prison. He died within months after being released in 1905. He was only sixty-four years old at the time.

Although not convicted, his wife, Helene, was implicated in the scandal. As with similar crimes

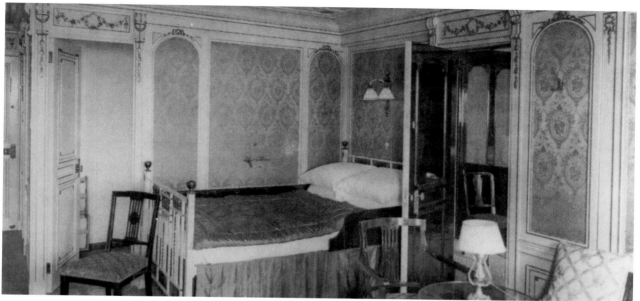

Baxter parlour suite Number 58 aboard Titanic

today, the question of the day had been "Where did all the money go?"

Despite the fall from grace, she was able to move her family into an expensive brownstone near McGill University, where they lived comfortably.

Ostracized from polite society, Helene started spending the winters in Europe. Each fall, at the beginning of the social season, she would depart for France. When the social season wound down in late spring, she would return.

Most reasoned that she was too embarrassed to socialize publicly. After all, she was from a well-respected, and well-heeled, old-school Quebecois family.

But the real reason for her annual trips to the Continent was likely to withdraw money stashed away in banks there by her late husband. The U.S. Department of Revenue had long been on his case,

stemming from a charge of violating currency exchange regulations, but the Feds were never able to make anything stick against either Diamond Jim or his wife.

In the fall of 1911, Quigg Baxter dropped out of his first year at McGill to accompany his mother to Europe. He was twenty-four years old at the time.

Big and strong, Baxter had spent his time after secondary private school mostly playing sports. He spent three years playing for the famed Montreal Shamrocks hockey team — it had won the Stanley Cup two years in a row, in 1899 and 1900 — but, in 1907, when Baxter was twenty years old, he lost an eye in a hockey game. That finished his dream of being a professional hockey player. From then on, most of his time was spent drinking and carousing.

In April of 1912, his sister, Mary Helene Douglas, who was married to a prominent Montreal doctor,

Baxter parlour suite Number 60 aboard Titanic

joined him and his mother in Paris to celebrate her twenty-seventh birthday. After Easter, Madame Baxter decided that it was time for all three to make the annual spring migration back to Montreal.

She booked them a suite of rooms aboard *Titanic*, the second-most expensive accommodations aboard ship. In today's value, they cost $140,000!

Unknown to Madame, though, her son had also bought his mistress/fiancée a first-class ticket under an assumed name. He had kept Berthe a secret those many months and clearly didn't intend to divulge the relationship to his mother, at least not just yet. Berthe's cabin was located one deck below the Baxters's, but was within easy walking distance. The Baxters and Mademoiselle de Villiers boarded *Titanic* when it stopped at Cherbourg, its second-last stop before heading out to sea on its maiden voyage.

The night of the disaster, despite being told personally by Captain Smith that everything was all right, Quigg Baxter quickly suspected otherwise. Soon after the collision with the iceberg, he had seen and heard Smith talking with Bruce Ismay, president of the White Star Line, outside his cabin. Ismay's cabin was next door to the Baxters's.

Quigg Baxter quickly bundled up his mother and sister and took them two decks up to *Titanic's* boat deck, depositing them in Lifeboat Number 6. It was the third lifeboat to depart the ship.

Then he returned for his lady love. At first, Berthe refused to leave his side. Only the insistence of another first-class passenger, the venerable and "unsinkable" Molly Brown, convinced her otherwise.

Quigg introduced Berthe to his mother and sister, for the first time, as he put her into their lifeboat. Lastly, he handed his mother a silver flask of

Colette

Born Sidonie-Gabrielle Colette, the cheeky bi-sexual was as famous for her antics off stage as on. She was linked romantically to American Josephine Baker, an infamous Parisian cabaret singer in her own right.

When performing at the Moulin Rouge in 1907, Colette kissed her co-performer "Missy" (Mathilde de Morny) on-stage. Their on-stage kiss nearly caused a riot and the police were called in to suppress it. The show was banned, but the incident only added to Colette's notoriety.

Colette in costume

She took lovers of both sexes, including an Italian writer and an automobile magnate. She married for the second time in 1912 and had a daughter, but she later divorced after a much-talked-about affair with her stepson.

In 1935, she married yet again.

In addition to being a talented cabaret performer, Colette was a prolific writer, respected artist and philanthropist.

She published over fifty novels, many with autobiographical elements. In 1927, she was proclaimed France's greatest woman writer. Her most enduring work is her novel *Gigi*, which was the basis for the Lerner & Loewe Broadway play and, later, Hollywood movie of the same name.

She also wrote and produced several operas for the Opera de Paris.

During World War I, she opened her country estate as a hospital for the wounded, and in 1920 she was made a Chevalier of the Legion of Honor for her efforts. Throughout World War II, she hid Jews in her home and secretly provided aid to others. For this, she was made a Grand Officer of the Legion of Honor in 1954.

When she died later that same year she was the first woman ever given a state funeral in France. However, she was refused Roman Catholic rites because she had been divorced.

Helene Baxter and daughter Mary

brandy and told all three to keep their spirits up as the boat was being lowered over the side. That was the last time they saw him.

Quigg Baxter's body was never recovered.

Berthe de Villiers stayed with Helene Baxter for several months. In the fall of 1912 she left for Paris, where she resumed her career on the stage under yet another new name, "Bella Veilly." Her newfound celebrity as a *Titanic* survivor opened the door for her with the city's best nightclubs, including the Moulin Rouge. She was even featured on the cover of a Paris fashion magazine in early 1913.

Sometime between the two World Wars, she returned to Belgium, where she settled in a comfortable suburb of Brussels. She never married — it was her nephew who found the shoebox.

Titanic Fashion

The time period from the beginning of the twentieth century until World War I is most often referred to as the "Edwardian Age," but in France it was known as the "Belle Epoque" or Beautiful Age.

It was a period of great social and technological change — characterized by many new innovations, discoveries and movements.

Women's fashion reflected this; the old-fashioned world of couture was being replaced by ready-to-wear, "pret-a-porter."

In London, the new department store Selfridges opened in 1909, providing off-the-rack fashionwear for the most discriminating tastes. That same year, Coco Chanel opened her first store in Paris.

Paris's great couture houses also reflected the changing styles of the age. Dyed fur was all the rage in 1912, especially skunk.

Eastern influences still prevailed at most fashion houses, including the use of the Persian tunic. Though some old styles were passé, such as the Japanese sleeve, some evolved, like the Japanese collar.

"It reaches high up over the ears where it is pulled out to give an almost square effect at the back. This leaves space for the lace ruffles of the dress beneath to be clearly visible, and to ensure them from being crushed," one fashion magazine of the time extolled.

The "V-neck" was introduced, along with the "Directorie-styled" empire line, which sat under the bust. Pastors at their pulpits railed against the V-neck.

By far the biggest change in women's clothes at the time was the dress itself. The new dance step, the Tango, was big on ballroom dance floors. Although dresses still were narrow at the ankle, they were looser-fitting and made of softer, and lighter, materials.

Upcoming woman designer Jeanne Farmant created dresses that were said to "cling to the form like a caress. It gives a woman a fine silhouette — divined rather than designed."

The height of new fashion for the time — the Blouse
Opposite page: Spring fashions 1912

Fabrics like chiffon and light silk were introduced but styles were still a long way off when it came to their many layers, as compared to today's standards. Dresses made from a single layer of fabric would not become fashionable until the 1920s.

A lace dinner dress has a chiffon underdress edged with a tiny plaited flounce, and over this a skirt of satin, or charmeuse, cut up at each side, the edges rounded. Over this is posed another skirt, composed of seven finely plaited narrow frills hung with small festoons of pearls, which is topped by a long wide sash, fastened in a big bow at the back and falling to the ground.

The back of the dinner gown and the afternoon frock were also more trimmed, typically taking the form of a big flat ribbon, knotted and looped into a small bow.

Such innovations didn't sit well with traditionalists such as designer Leon Bakst. He continued to make dresses in the Louis XV style. With their many layers these typically appealed to mostly older women (who wore corsets).

As a result, the fashion of the time was a collage of styles, colours and textures. This would have been reflected among the ladies in *Titanic*'s first class.

Against the white backdrop of the liner's luxury restaurants, dining saloons and reception rooms, the women's attire would have been an elegant kaleidoscope of colour and styles.

The dresses worn by younger women passengers would have been made of brightly coloured satin and chiffon and would have been embellished with jewelled trimmings and rich brocades.

Older women would have favoured more traditional black and white dresses, reflective of the late Victorian era. Those with more style would have chosen dresses featuring dark, rich velvets and other heavy, dark-coloured fabrics and materials. "Opium Grey" would have been a popular colour choice.

Hats were equally fashionable. Younger women may have opted for a Scotch cap of black velvet sporting a

Lady's walking suit
Opposite page: Evening gowns

single feather. Older women would have worn a wide-brimmed hat made of felt or straw and decorated with fur, ribbons, feathers and/or plumes.

DR. ALFRED PAIN
A Gentleman to the End

Known to his friends and family simply as "Alf," Dr. Alfred Pain was considered both a gentlemen and a scholar by everyone who knew him.

His father, Albert, was a retired army captain who had settled his family in Hamilton, Ontario. Before becoming a doctor, young Alf Pain was a well-known and well-liked athlete and musician. He played cricket and football in high school and was a crack shot with a rifle. He went on to become a member of the University of Toronto's champion varsity rifle team in 1909.

He was also a strong swimmer and a lover of water sports. He won several titles racing small sailboats at the Royal Hamilton Yacht Club, where his parents were members.

Next to sports, his other main leisure pursuit was music. He was said to have had "a critical ear" and was a gifted piano and flute player. He would often play or sing at home, sometimes accompanying his older brother, who was also a doctor, and his parents. His mother would play the piano and his father the violin. The family most often played chamber music and enjoyed singing hymns. His favourite was said to be the hymn "Nearer my God to Thee."

He was an accomplished choral performer, singing every Sunday in the choir of the Centenary Methodist Church, which his family attended. He played in that church's Sunday school orchestra and in the orchestra at St. John's Presbyterian Church, and he was a member of the Hamilton Symphony Club.

Pain studied medicine at the University of Toronto, enrolling there in 1906. As a member of the Class of 1910, at age twenty-one he was one of the youngest to ever graduate from the prestigious college.

He then spent a year as a medical resident at Hamilton City Hospital. One of his patients was his former high school principal, J. H. Collinson. Collinson later wrote that Pain had a wonderful bedside manner and that he greatly appreciated Pain's professionalism as a doctor.

The medical superintendent of City Hospital, Walter Langrill, later described Pain has having had a "lovable temperament" and many other sterling qualities.

Pain travelled to London in September 1911. There, he took a six-month post-graduate course studying surgical techniques.

Pain first tried to secure passage back to Canada as a ship's doctor. Unable to do so, and anxious to return home, he booked himself a second-class ticket aboard *Titanic*. An added incentive was that, aboard ship, there was an attractive young lady, Miss Marion Wright. They shared a mutual friend from London and had learned of each other's travel plans beforehand.

On Tuesday, April 9, Pain took the morning train down from London to Southampton with his cousin, who would see him off. They arrived mid-afternoon. After depositing Pain's trunks with the stationmaster, they toured around Southampton on foot — walking along the Strand River, crossing over Waterloo Bridge.

The next morning, Wednesday, April 10, the two men toured *Titanic* at the dockside.

"It was really splendid. I wished that I would go with him. He (Pain) was delighted. At last, I said goodbye and left the ship. As it sailed out I could see Alf standing on the deck waving to me," the cousin later wrote to Pain's parents.

Pain didn't meet up with Marion Wright until Friday, April 12, despite the fact that they were both travelling in second class. After that, they were often seen together — either dining or strolling along *Titanic*'s promenade deck.

Wright later described Pain as being affable and well-liked by other second-class passengers. Both attended church that Sunday in the second-class dining saloon. She played the organ and he sang in the impromptu choir during both the morning and afternoon services. That evening, they had dinner together with some of the others singers and then, after the evening's hymn-sing, which ended at 10 p.m., they retired to their separate cabins.

She later described *Titanic* hitting the iceberg that night as "a huge crash of glass." What alarmed her more was when the huge liner's engines stopped.

"It created such a painful silence. It inspired that something was not exactly right."

At first, she and her travelling companions were told by several of the ship's crew that there was nothing for them to worry about. But later, Wright found herself struggling in a crowd on *Titanic*'s boat deck. People were pushing and shoving, trying to put on lifebelts and to get into lifeboats.

Suddenly, Pain was there. He grabbed hold of her and guided her and her companions to one of the few remaining lifeboats, Lifeboat Number 9. She never got the chance to say goodbye to him.

As the lifeboat was lowered down, Alf Pain stood waving goodbye to Marion Wright. In less than an hour, *Titanic* would be gone. He was twenty-three years old. His body was never recovered.

There was a great outpouring of sympathy for the loss of the young doctor. Hundreds of cards and letters arrived at the home of his parents in Hamilton. They were too overcome with grief to respond, though. The job of replying to each and every one was left to Pain's older brother.

One letter stood out above all. It was from Marion Wright, now Marion Woolcott. Only days after *Titanic*'s sinking she had married her fiancé, Arthur Woolcott, and they had settled in Cottage Grove, Oregon, where Arthur had bought a farm. Also from England, he had emigrated to the U.S. in 1907.

He had learned of *Titanic*'s fate while travelling to New York to meet his bride-to-be. When Arthur arrived in the city, he learned that Marion had survived, but he missed her at dockside where the *Carpathia* had berthed. He searched several local hospitals and was eventually led to the home of Mr. and Mrs. Henry Milne on West 128th Street. When he rang their doorbell, it was Marion herself who answered.

Several days later, the couple wed. They then took a train to Oregon to start their new life together. Marion Woolcott wrote Alf Pain's parents from her new home.

In her letter, she described *Titanic*'s sinking. "The ship went down bit by bit until it broke in two and sank in a huge explosion," she wrote. The cries of the people in the water were heart-rending, she added.

As for Alf Pain, she said:

I had been on deck already for some time when your son came up — properly dressed and with his lifebelt on. I could see he had been looking for me.

"I've been trying to find you for some time," he said.

I asked him if he thought there was any great danger and he assured me that there wasn't.

We stood for some time on the starboard side, watching them load boats. There were hundreds of women and your son suddenly said: "I think we had better go round the other side; there aren't so many people there."

We did so, and scarcely had we got round when the call came, "Any more ladies, this way."

"You had better run," your son said.

I did so and he followed and put me in the lifeboat.

It is such a grief to me that I didn't say goodbye to him, but I thought, as everyone else did, that we would go back to the Titanic *before very long.*

When we got out on the scene we could see the boat gradually sinking, deck after deck. Oh, how much we hoped all would be saved before she went down.

But when the awful news came to us, that only 700 were saved, and those were with us on the Carpathia, *how grieved I felt and how I wished your son had been among us.*

It all seems so sad and overwhelming and I will never forget it as long as I live.

Marion and Arthur Woolcott were married for fifty-three years and had three sons. Marion died in 1965 at age eighty.

Music That Fateful Night

Titanic's *orchestra*

After dinner on Sunday evening, April 14, 1912, each of *Titanic*'s three classes of passengers celebrated in their own way.

Far below deck in the third-class dining saloon an impromptu party was underway, with music provided by fellow passengers.

There were two musical ensembles aboard *Titanic* for its first-class passengers: a five-piece orchestra and a three-string trio, both under the direction of bandmaster and violinist Wallace Hartley. *Titanic*'s elite were greeted by music performed by the quintet as they gathered in the first-class dining saloon's reception room. Once dinner began, Hartley's group moved into the dining saloon and played appropriate background selections.

After dinner, they returned to the reception room and gave a concert, closing with selections from Offen-bach's *The Tales of Hoffmann.*

None of *Titanic*'s eight musicians survived, so it's impossible to know exactly what songs they played that fateful night.

Many tunes would have been from the White Star Line's music book. It was heavy with grand operas, including French, Italian and German composers. Wagner's Tannhäuser was popular at the time. Lighter comic fare, such as selections from Sir Arthur Sullivan's opera *The Mikado*, was also included.

With over 350 tunes in the book, the musical styles of the day were well-reflected. Jazz was all the rage in America. Survivors remember hearing the Irving Berlin tune "Alexander's Ragtime Band" as the ship sank. Waltzes were also popular at the time and were played that night, before and during the sinking.

HARRY MARKLAND MOLSON

There Was No Swimming Away This Time

Harry Molson was the great-grandson of the famed Canadian brewer John Molson. The latter had founded North America's oldest brewery in 1786 after immigrating to Canada from England. By 1817 he also owned a fleet of five steamships, which his company built from scratch. They plied the waters of the St. Lawrence River. In 1850 John Molson started the Molson Bank, which later became the Bank of Montreal.

Harry Molson was born in 1856, the son of William and Helen Molson. After attending secondary private school in Montreal, he spent four years in Europe attending different universities in France and Germany. He dropped out of them all, never earning a degree — academics were not his strong suit.

Despite this, because of his family's name and reputation he ended up serving on the board of directors for several important companies such as the Standard Chemical, Iron and Lumber Company of Canada (his friend, and fellow yachtsman, Major Arthur Peuchen from Toronto was its president).

When his uncle "Jackey" (John Henry Robinson Molson) died in 1897, Harry Molson succeeded him as chairman of the Molson Bank as well as inheriting most of his uncle's fortune. Jackey Molson, the favourite grandson of patriarch John Molson, had inherited the Molson Brewery from the Old Man in 1847. He also had financial interests in the Montreal Street Railway, the City and District Bank and the Scottish Life Assurance Company. Jackey and his wife, Louisa Goddard Frothingham, the daughter of a wealthy hardware entrepreneur, had no children of their own and left their sizable wealth to their favourite nephew, Harry.

Harry Molson was best known for his love of the good life and his wild ways. He belonged to a number of private clubs in Montreal, like the St. James Club, the Jockey Club and The Royal. He was also a member of Montreal's Golf and Country Club.

When in London, England, he frequented the prestigious Athenaeum Club, which still exists today. The club boasts fifty-two Nobel prizewinners as either current or past members. It's said that the club was founded as a meeting place for men who enjoy "the life of the mind." Author Charles Dickens and naturalist Charles Darwin were both members. It opened its doors to women for the first time in 2002.

Harry Molson was particularly fond of sailboat racing. When not at the helm of his yacht *Redcoat*, he could often be found ashore, with drink in hand, at Montreal's St. Lawrence Yacht Club. There, he was better known as "Merry" Molson. He served as the yacht club's commodore from 1900 to 1902. In 1901, Molson won the Lord Strathcona's Challenge Cup aboard *Redcoat*. The year before, he won the Seawanhaka International Challenge Cup at Lake St. Louis in the U.S.

A life-long bachelor, Molson divided his time between his Westmount home in Montreal, at 2 Edgehill Avenue, and his summer home in Dorval, today's 960 Lakeside Drive. When not there, which was most of the time, he could be found aboard his luxury steam yacht, the seventy-six-foot (twenty-five-metre) *Alcyone*, and he wasn't often alone!

Rumour within Montreal's elite social circle had it that he was part of an incestuous love triangle involving his cousin Alexander Morris and his wife Florence. Gossips said that Mrs. Morris was often aboard ship alone with Molson.

What's known for sure is that Harry Molson changed his will before his last trip to Europe, leav-

Molson Bank

ing Florence close to $1,000,000 (at today's value).

Despite his playboy ways, Molson was a popular politician. He was a Montreal city alderman and he was the town of Dorval's first mayor.

He was a humanitarian and philanthropist. He followed in his uncle's footsteps, becoming the governor of Montreal's General Hospital. He was also the president of the Canadian Society for the Prevention of Cruelty to Animals.

Molson sat on the board of directors for several companies in addition to his friend's company, Standard Chemical. In February 1912, he travelled to England on business. He was originally booked to return to Canada aboard another liner, the *Tunisian*, at the end of March, but his friend,

Titanic *at night*

Arthur Peuchen, persuaded him otherwise.

Peuchen planned to sail aboard *Titanic* on its maiden voyage the following month. His chemical company operated a number of refineries in Europe and he was a regular traveller to and from the Continent. In fact, his trip aboard the world's newest and biggest liner was to be his fortieth crossing of the North Atlantic. He told his friend Harry that it was an opportunity not to be missed.

Molson altered his travel plans accordingly. He was the wealthiest Canadian aboard the great ship.

Sunday night, April 14, 1912, the two friends had dinner together along with Hud and Bess Allison from Montreal. Mr. Allison was a stock broker and businessman who had a reputation for being a sharp investor. The Allisons were travelling with their two small children and several servants.

Shortly after 9 p.m., the group adjourned from *Titanic*'s first-class dining saloon and returned to their respective cabins. Peuchen stopped in at the first-class smoking room to have a drink and

a cigar with some friends from Winnipeg. Around 11:20 p.m. he returned to his cabin on C Deck.

Sometime after the collision with the iceberg, Peuchen saw Molson topside on *Titanic*'s boat deck.

Molson also had the reputation for being lucky when it came to surviving shipwrecks. Twice before he had swum to safety in the St. Lawrence — in 1899 when the *Scotsman* went down and again in 1904 when the liner *Canada* collided with the collier *Sorel*.

He was last seen removing his shoes, preparing to swim to a ship seen off *Titanic*'s port bow.

Unfortunately for him, the *Californian* appeared much closer than it actually was, most likely because of unusual atmospheric conditions. Instead of being a mile away, the phantom tramp steamer was likely closer to ten miles (sixteen kilometres) off.

Harry Molson's body was never recovered.

Immersion Hypothermia

Harry Molson wouldn't have survived in the water for very long, no matter how strong a swimmer he was. In fact, he may not have even survived his plunge into the freezing water — around thirty-two degrees Fahrenheit (F), zero degrees Celsius (C).

According to the United States Search and Rescue Task Force, the initial shock of diving or jumping into water that cold can place a severe strain on the body, going so far as to produce instant cardiac arrest. This has happened with individuals as young as fifteen; Molson was fifty-five years old.

In addition to the shock, there's also the risk of a person panicking and drowning. Survivors of cold-water accidents have reported their breath being driven from them when they first entered the water. If the person's face is underwater when they involuntarily try to breathe, it can cause the person to also panic. Panic-stricken persons have reported thrashing helplessly in the water for thirty seconds or more, totally disoriented, until they're able to get their bearings.

Immersion in cold water can quickly numb the extremities to the point of uselessness. Cold hands cannot fasten the straps of a lifejacket or hold onto anything such as an overturned lifeboat. Within minutes, severe pain clouds rational thought and hypothermia sets in.

The body's normal temperature is 98.6 degrees F (37 degrees C). Shivering and the sensation of cold can begin when the body's temperature lowers to approximately 96.5 degrees F (35.8 degrees C). Amnesia can begin to set in at approximately 94 degrees F (34 degrees C), unconsciousness at 86 degrees F (30 degrees C) and death at approximately 79 degrees F (26 degrees C).

Dr. Alan Steinman is a retired U.S. Coast Guard rear admiral and the former director of health and safety for the U.S. Coast Guard and remains a consultant to the U.S.C.G. for issues of sea-survival, hypothermia and

Preparing bodies aboard the **Minia**

drowning. According to him, Harry Molson's survival time swimming without a lifebelt would have been thirty minutes or less.

The survival time for a *Titanic* victim wearing a lifebelt would have depended on their body type and size and what they were wearing. Unconsciousness would likely have occurred within one to two hours after entering the water, says Steinman.

Size and Distance Mattered

One of the lesser-known details of the tragedy is that another ship, the *Californian*, lay nearby from the time *Titanic* hit the iceberg until it sank a little less than three hours later. Despite seeing eight white rockets fired in succession by *Titanic*, the *Californian* did not come to the foundering liner's aid. If it had, it likely could have saved many lives.

Since Titanic's sinking, there's been much study and speculation as to how far apart the two ships actually were, and whether the *Californian* had been close enough to rescue anyone aboard *Titanic*.

Around 7 p.m. Sunday evening, while steaming west towards America, the *Californian* encountered several large icebergs. As the evening progressed, the tramp steamer encountered more and more ice westward. Shortly after 10 p.m., Captain Stanley Lord gave the order to stop for the night. His ship would wait it out until daylight, when it would be safer to resume travel.

The *Californian*'s wireless operator, Cyril Evans, shut off his Marconi set at 11:30 p.m. and turned in for the night. It wasn't until 5:30 a.m. Monday, when Evans came back on duty, that the crew of the *Californian* learned of *Titanic*'s fate. By then it was too late for them to do anything.

On arrival in Boston, Lord first told one newspaper that his ship had been thirty miles (fifty kilometres) from *Titanic*. He later told another that *Titanic* had been more like twenty miles off. Several of the *Californian*'s crew later testified that their ship had likely been less than ten miles away.

Officers on both ships tried to contact the other with the use of Morse hand lamps, to no avail. Aboard *Titanic*, Fourth Officer Joseph Boxhall estimated the other ship to be five miles off his ship's bow.

The ship appeared so close that Captain Smith actually ordered the first several lifeboats away to steer for it. The lights of the ship were seen from *Titanic*'s lifeboats throughout the night. One lifeboat did try to row towards it but the phantom eluded it, never getting any closer.

Nor did the *Californian* see the rockets, coincidentally fired by the same Officer Boxhall in Lifeboat Number 2 at 4 a.m. But it did see the rockets fired by the rescue vessel *Carpathia*, which lay approximately ten miles (sixteen kilometres) to the south of Boxhall's position.

According to several experts, both in 1912 and over the years, the green signal rockets fired from Lifeboat Number 2 would likely have been visible seven to ten miles away.

As author Daniel Allen Butler wrote in *The Other Side of the Night*: "The crime of Stanley Lord was not that he may have ignored *Titanic*'s rockets, but that he, unquestionably, ignored its cry for help." All Lord had to do was wake Evans up and get him to turn on his wireless set to find out what was up with the other vessel.

One of the experts, Captain John Knapp of the U.S. Hydrographic Office, also testified at the U.S. inquiry in 1912 that the curvature of the earth (the horizon) would have prevented either ship from seeing the other if they were more than sixteen miles (twenty-six kilometres) apart.

This meant, according to Captain Knapp, that the *Californian* must have been between seven and sixteen miles (between eleven and twenty-six kilometres) away from *Titanic* the whole time.

But, the U.S. board of inquiry concluded, based on additional evidence and testimony, that the ships were, in fact, eighteen miles (thirty kilometres) apart.

Some later re-examinations put the two ships even further apart. In 1992, the government of the United Kingdom instructed its Marine Accident Investigation Branch to review the matter. It had the advantage of knowing where *Titanic* actually sank. The wreck had been found in 1985 by a joint French/American expedition led by Dr. Robert Ballard. The location of the stern section of *Titanic* was found to be thirteen miles (twenty-one kilometres) from the accepted position of

Athenaeum Club, London

the ship's sinking.

Combined with additional insight about sea currents at the time of *Titanic*'s loss, Captain P. B. Marriott, chief inspector of marine accidents, stated on March 12, 1992, that the Marine Accident Investigation Branch's official position was "that the *Californian* was between 17 to 20 miles from *Titanic* at the time of collision" and that "between the collision and sinking, both ships will, in all probability, have drifted similarly so that their position, relative to each other, would not appreciably change."

The 1992 report remains the British government's official position regarding the *Californian*.

So, why then did both ships appear much closer to each other than they actually were — if this was, in fact, the case?

The 1992 British reappraisal offered up one interesting possibility — super refraction. Also known as "downward refraction," this meteorological condition occurs when air at sea level is colder (and, therefore,

more dense) than air higher up. It creates a "superior mirage" where distant objects appear to float above the horizon, and objects that are below the horizon may come into view. This can also result in the object appearing to be stretched as well as elevated.

Objects that appear bigger often appear closer. This is especially true at sea, where there are no fixed reference points that an observer can use to judge distance and compare size — even more so at night.

The 1992 British report also stated that, had the *Californian* responded appropriately, the freighter wouldn't have arrived on scene any sooner than the *Carpathia* did — roughly two hours after *Titanic* sank.

Of course, others disagree. Even at twenty miles (twenty-eight kilometres) away, the *Californian* was less than half as far from *Titanic* as *Carpathia* had been at midnight, when *Titanic* broadcast its first distress message. *Carpathia* was then fifty-eight miles (ninety-three kilometres) to the south, and closed that distance in under four hours.

ALICE FORTUNE
Debutantes & Gentlemen

The Fortune family of Winnipeg was returning from a three-month "Grand Tour" of Europe — a popular wintertime diversion for the wealthy of the era. Mark Fortune, Alice's father, was a prominent property developer, responsible for erecting most of the new city's commercial buildings downtown.

Originally from Ontario, Fortune moved around a lot as a young man, learning the ways of the world and how to make money. While still in his late teens, he made it all the way to San Francisco!

In 1871, when he was only twenty-four years old, he arrived in Manitoba. Sensing opportunity, the enterprising young man bought land on the banks of the Assiniboine River — land which would later become Winnipeg's main street, Portage Avenue.

He was an active member of the Knox Presbyter-

ian Church and of the St. Charles Country Club. He served as the president of the St. Andrew's Society of Winnipeg, and he was the founder of the Winnipeg Real Estate Board. He served on Winnipeg City Council for several years and, in 1886, ran as the Liberal candidate in the Woodlands Constituency, though he didn't win.

Affable and well-liked, Mark Fortune was also said to have been the city's best curler.

In 1911, he built a thirty-six-room mansion on Wellington Crescent. It still stands today.

Travelling with Fortune was his wife, Mary, son, Charles, and daughters, Alice, Ethel and Mabel. He had waited until the youngest, "Charlie," had finished secondary school. The trip was a "coming-out event" of sorts.

Nineteen-year-old Charles had recently graduated from Bishop's College in Lennoxville, Que-

Cruise passengers at the Sphinx

bec, and was planning to enter McGill University that fall.

Like the Baxters from Montreal, the Fortunes occupied one of *Titanic*'s two expensive parlour suites. Theirs was located on the ship's starboard side.

Travelling first-class with the Fortunes were three family friends. Two were considered Winnipeg's most eligible bachelors: Hugo Ross, a real estate developer, and Thomson Beattie, a railroad contractor. The other of the trio was Thomas McCaffry. He had lived in Winnipeg before moving to Vancouver to become the manager of the Union Bank's branch there.

Together, the entire group reflected the wealthy and privileged of the Edwardian Era. By the end of the nineteenth century, Winnipeg had become the commercial distribution centre for the Canadian West. At the time of *Titanic*'s sinking, it was said that the upstart city had more millionaires per capita than any other city in North America. The year after, 1913, was the high-water mark for immigration to Canada, and most settlers headed west through Winnipeg.

The Fortune entourage travelled first to New York by train, where they boarded the Cunard liner *Franconia*. From there, they sailed to Trieste, Italy, which in those days was the main seaport of the Austro-Hungarian Empire.

They leisurely toured the classical sites of Italy and Greece, the great pyramids of Egypt, the chateaus of France and the castles of England. Their tour ended in London, where they spent Easter. On Wednesday morning, April 10, 1912, they took the train to Southampton to board *Titanic*, the vessel that was to take them home to North America. It departed at noon.

Alice seated at the wheel of a car with friends

door. It was young Charlie Fortune. He said that he was going up on deck to find out what had happened. Later, he returned and told his mother that the ship had hit an iceberg.

The women hurriedly dressed and went out into the hallway. Despite being told by stewards that there was nothing to worry about, and to go back to bed, they made their way up to the ship's boat deck. Along the way, they met up with Mark Fortune, who joined them, but at the stairway to the boat deck they were stopped by a group of officers who told them that only the women could pass. Both Mark and Charlie Fortune stayed behind.

They (the women) didn't even have time to say goodbye, Allen told the reporter. "One of the Fortune sisters called out to their younger brother, saying 'look after Father.'"

The Fortune women were placed in Lifeboat Number 10, which was under the command of Second Officer Charles Lightoller.

Mary Fortune remembered that it was terribly overcrowded. It was the tenth lifeboat to leave *Titanic*, she told her future son-in-law. Actually, it was the seventh out of twenty boats, departing at 1:20 a.m.

Gentlemen to a fault, Mark Fortune (age sixty-four) and his son, Charlie, died in the sinking, as did all three of their male friends. Only the bodies of two were recovered; Thomson Beattie was buried at sea and Thomas McCaffry's body was sent to Montreal for burial. Mark and Charlie Fortune's bodies were not recovered.

Alice's fiancé Charles Allen, also of Winnipeg, met her, her mother (age sixty), and her sisters, Ethel (age twenty-eight) and Mabel (age twenty-three), when they arrived in New York aboard the *Carpathia*. They all checked into the Belmont Hotel.

The Fortune women wouldn't talk to reporters, saying that it was too painful, so Charles Allen spoke for them. He told a reporter from the *New York Times* that the women had been asleep in their cabin when *Titanic* hit the iceberg.

Mrs. Mary Fortune described the collision as a "violent shiver;" then they heard a knock on the

Mrs. Fortune was of the opinion that no discrimination was made between (women) passengers of the first, second or third class in making allotments for seats in the boats.

When several men in steerage tried to rush the officers in charge, the officers slugged them (with their fists).

Passengers grew more terrified.

Then, the officers made use of their revolvers, first firing them in the air. Next, they aimed them at the men.

Around 2:30 a.m. *Titanic* sank.

Alice was a great socializer, as shown in a photo from the 1930s

They saw the stern hoist itself in the air. A crowd could be seen struggling. Shrieks came across the water.

After *Titanic* was gone, Lightoller steered his boat in the dark to meet up with Lifeboats 4, 12, 14 and Collapsible D to more evenly distribute passengers. Then, Lifeboat Number 14, under the command of Fifth Officer Harold Lowe, returned to the wreck site to look for more survivors. He found only four men alive.

As dawn broke, Lowe came upon Lifeboat Collapsible A, which was almost full of water. He rescued a dozen survivors.

On Monday, April 21, 1912, the Fortunes boarded a railroad passenger car arranged by the Canadian Pacific Railway and returned to Winnipeg with other Canadian *Titanic* survivors.

Ethel Fortune was haunted for the rest of her life because of what she saw the night *Titanic* sank. She had a recurring nightmare of her brother, Charlie, flailing about in the freezing water, crying for someone to save him.

Alice Fortune married Charles Allen on June 8, 1912. They had a daughter, Mary.

Charles became a lawyer and practised law for some years in Fredericton, New Brunswick. He later became the assistant to the manager and director of the National Surety Company in Montreal.

The couple bought a vacation home in Chester, Nova Scotia. It was there they retired.

Alice Allen died on April 7, 1961, and was buried in the Chester cemetery.

Cuisine a la Titanic

Lamb, an entree similar to what would have been served to first-class passengers

The *Titanic* had three formal dining rooms, one for each class of passenger. Each was staffed by White Star employees and served a fixed menu that changed daily.

First-class passengers could also avail themselves of the ship's A La Carte Restaurant, an independent concession that was manned by a dedicated staff with its own kitchen. Its manager was Luigi Gatti, who had been hired away from London's prestigious Imperial Restaurant. Before that, he had worked at the famous Ritz Hotel.

When it came to choosing his executive chef, there was only one man for the job — Pierre Rousseau. He had worked for Gatti in London before he signed on-board the *Olympic*. When *Titanic* sailed, Gatti made sure Rousseau was aboard working for him.

The A La Carte Restaurant was modelled after the greatest dining rooms of Europe's best grand hotels. It offered a wide range of spectacular dishes, hence its name. Meals were served on the best china, by first-rate waiters, in the most opulent surroundings.

In fact, some passengers nicknamed the restaurant "the Ritz" because it so resembled London's premier eatery. Other well-travelled passengers may also have been familiar with the "Ritz rooms" aboard the ocean liners of the Hamburg-Amerika Line.

Because there was no fixed menu, it's impossible to know for sure what the likes of Captain Smith ate that fateful Sunday night — their last meal.

No doubt, it consisted of hors d'oeuvres, followed by soup, likely a consommé, which was followed by a fish dish, possibly poached salmon. Entrees, such as Tournedos aux Morilles (medallions of beef served with morel mushrooms in a red wine sauce), were likely served next.

The meal's main course would most likely have been an oven-cooked dish. Some survivors remembered eating roasted squab, which was served in *Titanic*'s first-class dining saloon. Others remembered being served lobster in a rich cream sauce.

Regardless, the main entree would have been served with a cold salad, which would likely have featured a vinaigrette dressing, and cooked vegetables, such as asparagus (which was then a delicacy).

"We dined the last night in the Ritz restaurant. It was the last word in luxury. The tables were gay with pink roses and white daisies, the women in their beautiful shimmering gowns of satin and silk, the men immaculate and well-groomed, the stringed orchestra playing music from Puccini and Tchaikovsky. The food was superb: caviar, lobster, quail from Egypt, plover's eggs,

Preparing a delectable gravy

and hothouse grapes and fresh peaches," remembered first-class passenger Mrs. Walter Douglas.

The meal would have concluded with desserts like Waldorf Pudding, Peaches in Chartreuse Jelly and Chocolate-painted Eclairs with French Vanilla Cream. Frozen "American-style" ice cream would have been a particular favourite with the younger set.

After their fine meal, diners would have retired to the reception room, outside the restaurant, for coffee and/or a drink of port or liqueur.

From there, the women would have retired to their cabins for the evening. Most men in first class, on the other hand, would have made their way to the Georgian-style smoking room for a drink and cigar. It was strictly "men only," imitating a private men's club. There, men would visit and converse about politics, business and (what else) women!

BEHIND THE SCENES

It took an army to prepare and serve each day's three meals for all three classes, plus the assorted snacks and light meals that were offered. Just like an army, it took a great deal of planning, coordination and attention to detail for things to go smoothly.

Baker Charles Burgess felt *Titanic* hit the iceberg, but it didn't stop him or the other bakers from working. When the ship hit, some pans of rolls fell off the counter and were scattered on the main galley's floor. Chief night baker Walter Belford cursed, told one of his assistants to clean up the mess, and began to make more dough.

Burgess removed some bread from the oven, replacing it with a batch of scones. His next job was to make cornbread, a breakfast favourite with the ship's American passengers, but just before midnight, before he could start, the call came, "All hands on deck."

Most dining room stewards, like second-class dining room steward William Ryerson, wouldn't have been long in their bunks when the collision occurred, if they were there at all. Typically, their long day started before

Afternoon Tea

6 a.m. in their dormitory on E Deck. When not serving passengers in their assigned dining room, a steward usually assisted in other public rooms, perhaps serving beef broth on deck, or afternoon tea, to first- and second-class passengers.

The dining rooms closed at 10 p.m. The stewards helped clean up and prepare the great room for the next day, replacing table linens and setting the tables with silver and glassware. The same was repeated when the first- and second-class lounges closed at 11 p.m. A steward was lucky to be in his bed before midnight.

BREAKFAST

During *Titanic*'s trip, morning tea was set out at 7 a.m.

for first- and second-class passengers. It consisted of tea and coffee, fresh-baked pastries served with jam and marmalade, and fruit. First-class passengers could also have theirs delivered to their cabin.

At 8 a.m., the breakfast bugle was sounded and passengers of all classes made their way to the ship's three dining rooms (saloons).

Edwardians had huge appetites by today's standards.

For breakfast, first-class passengers ate copious quantities of food, both hot and cold, including grilled ham, fish, sausage and mutton served with eggs cooked in a variety of styles, and potatoes — boiled, mashed or fried. Pork or beef steaks were available on request.

Fruit dishes, such as stewed prunes and baked apples, were served along with fresh fruit. Dry cereals and porridge were offered. There was a mountain of rolls, scones, breads and pastries, served with jams, various types of honey and marmalade.

At 10 a.m. breakfast concluded. That last Sunday there was a church service, which started at 10:30 a.m. in both the first- and second-class dining rooms.

By the standards of the day, *Titanic*'s third-class passengers also enjoyed exceptional cuisine. For breakfast, they were served a hearty meal, which included smoked herring and tripe served with boiled potatoes. Only a few years before, steerage passengers had been required to bring their own food.

DINNER

At 1 p.m. the bugle sounded again, calling passengers to dinner. In the second-class dining saloon cold meats, salads and a variety of cheeses were served.

A number of hot entrees were also available each day, including spaghetti au gratin, corned beef with dumplings, and roast mutton with baked potatoes.

The meal concluded with dessert, tapioca pudding

Dressed salmon

or an apple tart, and fresh fruit followed by coffee.

First-class passengers were offered a meal similar to those in second class, but with even finer entrees served.

The midday meal was the big meal of the day for third-class passengers. Soup was served first, followed by a choice of entree, such as curried mutton and rice, baked rabbit or corned beef and cabbage, served with cooked peas and boiled potatoes. For dessert, they were served pudding with sauce or fresh fruit, typically oranges.

Instead of supper, third-class passengers were served evening tea. It consisted of a single entree like grilled mutton, roast beef, rabbit pie or fried fish, served with a simple dessert, such as apples and rice. There was plenty of bread and jam, washed down with tea.

For those not already stuffed, a light late supper of biscuits and cheese followed by soup and coffee was served before bedtime at 10 p.m. Right up until the very end, no one on *Titanic*, not even its lowest-class passengers, went hungry.

THE MAIN EVENT

For first- and second-class passengers, the day's big event was their evening meal. Sunday suppers were extra special aboard all liners of the day, and *Titanic* was no exception.

In second class, diners were offered a three-course meal. It started with soup, consommé with tapioca. Next, diners could choose their entree. They had four to choose from: baked haddock with sharp sauce, curried chicken and rice, lamb with mint sauce, or roast turkey with cranberry sauce. Each meal was served with steamed green peas, turnip purée and the diner's choice of either roast or boiled potatoes.

For the third course, dessert, second-class diners could choose from plum pudding with sweet sauce, wine jelly, a coconut sandwich (cookies with coconut cream in between) or American ice cream. Assorted nuts, fresh fruit, cheeses and biscuits were also served with coffee.

By far the most extravagant meal aboard *Titanic* that last night was the one served in the first-class dining saloon. It was an eleven-course affair.

Top: Lobster Thermidor
Middle: Pigeon with nettle risotto
Bottom: Rabbit and skordalia

Chef Charles Proctor and his battalion of kitchen staff had outdone themselves. One first-class passenger, Major Arthur Peuchen from Toronto, described the evening's meal as being "exceptionally good!"

At 6 p.m. the bugle sounded for first-class passengers to dress.

The evening's "main event" began with hors d' oeuvres: Oysters à la Russe (raw oysters), and Canapés a l'Amiral (shrimp butter and caviar from flying fish, served on broiled French bread).

Next, diners chose a soup: either Consomme Olga (Russian-style vegetable soup), or cream of barley.

The third course was poached salmon with a sauce of Hollandaise and whipped cream, garnished with sliced cucumbers.

For their fourth course, first-class passengers had three choices: Filets Mignons Lili (beef filets accompanied by a buttery wine sauce, topped with foie gras and truffles set on a bed of fried potatoes), Chicken Lyonnaise (fried chicken served with onions in a white wine sauce) or Vegetable Marrow Farci (baked yellow squash stuffed with savoury rice and mushrooms).

Again, diners had a choice for the fifth course. They could choose from roasted lamb, duck or beef, served with baked potatoes, cream carrots and green peas.

The sixth course was the beverage Punch Romaine. Served as a palate cleanser, it was made from champagne, white wine and light rum mixed with orange peels and lemon juice.

The seventh course, the roast, was broiled squab (a small game bird like a Cornish game hen or partridge) served on wilted watercress.

The eighth course was the salad. That night's was Asparagus Salad with Champagne-Saffron Vinaigrette. The vinaigrette was made with saffron threads, champagne or white wine vinegar and extra virgin olive oil, spiced with Dijon mustard.

The ninth course, the cold dish, was chilled Pâté de

Foie Gras served with celery.

The tenth course was the sweets, which we'd call the dessert course today. Diners could choose from Waldorf Pudding (apple pudding with walnuts, raisins and apples), Peaches in Chartreuse Jelly (poached peaches in fruit gelatin), Chocolate-painted Eclairs with French Vanilla Cream or "French-style" Vanilla Ice Cream.

After her husband became president in 1809, Dolly Madison popularized the consumption of ice cream in the U.S., but, unlike on the Continent, her recipe didn't include eggs. The French preferred theirs with eggs because it made the ice cream richer and smoother.

The meal's eleventh course, the "dessert," consisted of assorted nuts, fresh fruits and cheeses.

After dinner, coffee (with fine cigars for the gentlemen) was served in the restaurant's reception room.

Different wines, selected to complement the food, were served with each course, with the exception of the last. With it, port, liqueurs or hard-liquor cocktails were served.

A UNIQUE VIEW

The dishes in these photographs were prepared by Miles Collins, head chef of the, Branston Hall Country House Hotel in Lincoln, England, and executive chef for a group of hotels and resorts across Europe. Prior to this, he was a chef at a number of hotels in the United Kingdom and Germany.

Top right: Tray service
Bottom right: Sorbet and jelly

Titanic Tableware

Russ Upholster is a leading authority on the china patterns used on *Titanic*. According to him, much of *Titanic*'s china bore the mark "Stonier Co. Liverpool" on its reverse side. Stonier and Company didn't actually make the china, though; it was only the distributor. Much of the china aboard *Titanic*, especially those pieces used in second and third class, was actually made by a company called Bisto. The White Star Line purchased high-end china produced by Spode and Royal Crown Derby. Spode purchased many of its newer designs at the time from the pottery house of William Brownfield and Son, which was out of business by the beginning of the twentieth century.

CROWN PATTERN
FIRST-CLASS DINING & RECEPTION ROOM, FIRST-CLASS CABIN SERVICE & VERANDAH CAFÉS

Originally made by Brownfield in 1882, the larger dinner plates featured a turquoise-and-brown arched pattern, referred to as "Crown." By the time *Titanic* sailed, the service was being made by Spode. Smaller dishes, such as side plates and teacup saucers, and other pieces of tableware, such as teacups, creamers, sugar bowls, milk jugs and others, didn't have the arches. Some smaller pieces also had a "brown-on-brown" colour scheme with no turquoise. This was fine bone china and it broke easily.

ROYAL CROWN DERBY PATTERN
A LA CARTE RESTAURANT

This style of service was used exclusively in *Titanic*'s A La Carte Restaurant. The pattern reflected the "swag" style of decoration used on the restaurant's ceiling light fixtures.

It was made by Royal Crown Derby. The company used *Titanic* as a backdrop to promote the pattern. Dinner sets were sold in stores with an advertising card showing an exterior image of *Titanic*. On the inside was a photograph of the first-class dining room from its sister ship, *Olympic*.

GREEK KEY PATTERN
CAFÉ PARISIEN

Manufactured by Spode, commonly referred to as the "Greek Key" pattern, it was popular with White Star Line ships and was used from 1911 to at least 1933. It was one of the pottery firm's most prestigious cobalt blue patterns. It's believed to have been used in *Titanic*'s Café Parisien.

SPECIAL SERVICE PATTERN
PARLOUR SUITES

The most expensive china aboard *Titanic*, it was likely only used in the ship's two Empire suites and four Parlour suites. It may also have been intended as a luncheon service for VIP guests.

Another of Spode's Cobalt series, it was mostly dark blue in colour with gold accents. It was referred to as the "Boston" pattern. Today, Spode makes a nearly identical one called "Lancaster."

GILDED RIM PATTERN
DECK SERVICE, FIRST & SECOND CLASSES

Simple and attractive, this style of white china was heavier than other first-class ware. It featured a two-colour White Star logo with a gold rim. Because only a few pieces have been found, and because of its rugged design, it's believed that it wasn't used as a full table service. Instead, it was likely used on deck to serve passengers hot chocolate and beef broth.

FLOW BLUE PATTERN
SECOND-CLASS DINING ROOM

This was a very attractive pattern of restaurant-grade china that was made by several pottery houses of the day, including Minton, Bisto and Foley, and brokered by

Stonier Company. The style, also called Delft Blue, got its name from the city of Delft, Holland. Originally made in China, popular blue-on-white housewares had been marketed from there since the early 1700s. In England, Wedgewood is credited for introducing the "Flow Blue" pattern in 1820.

COMMON PATTERN
THIRD-CLASS DINING ROOM

This was simple white-ware, also called "open stock," with the White Star Line logo in the middle printed in maroon. Unlike the unique hand-painted china used in *Titanic*'s first-class areas, it was mass-produced and was also used on other White Star ships of the day.

Some third-class pieces of the same common pattern on *Titanic* also featured a maroon rim. This fancier version may have been used for second class on other White Star ships.

GLASSWARE

In first class, the glassware was hand-cut lead crystal which had the White Star burgee etched on it. There were also crystal-glass wine and water carafes, liquor decanters, fruit bowls and flower vases with the White Star flag also on them.

Second and third classes used mass-produced glassware that had the White Star burgee etched on it.

FLATWARE

The silverplate "Reed and Star" pattern cutlery used by *Titanic*'s first-class passengers was most likely produced by Elkington, which had taken over the manufacturing silversmiths Henry Wilkinson & Company in 1892. It merged with Mappin & Web in the 1960s, becoming British Silverware Lim-

ited, but that conglomerate went under in 1971.

Titanic's second- and third-class passengers used silverware that had a plain pattern, with the White Star burgee on it. Smaller pieces such as teaspoons were likely also used in first class, because the silverware's size was too small for it to be made in the Reed and Star pattern.

LOUNGES AND SMOKING SALOONS (FIRST AND SECOND CLASSES)

Glassware would have been used predominantly in *Titanic*'s smoking saloons.

The china used in the ship's lounges and smoking salons was likely the same as that used in the dining salons of the same class. Using similar china would make sense, given their close proximity to one another.

ARTHUR PEUCHEN
Big Mouth at the Big Event

Despite his middle-class roots, Arthur Godfrey Peuchen became an influential international chemist and one of Canada's wealthiest men. He was born in Montreal in 1859, the son of immigrants. His father was a railroad contractor. His parents wanted the best for their son and enrolled him in Montreal's best private schools.

At twenty-two years of age, he joined the militia in Toronto, serving with the Queens Own Rifles, first as a lieutenant. Originally named the Second Battalion, Volunteer Militia Rifles of Canada, the regiment changed its name after the Battle of Ridgeway during the Fenian Raids of 1886. Members also fought in the North-West Rebellion of 1885 and during the South African War (the Boer War) from 1899 to 1900. It exists today as a part of the Reserves of the Canadian Armed Forces.

He was later promoted to the rank of captain, then major, and finally lieutenant-colonel (after the *Titanic* disaster). In 1911, he served as the marshalling officer for the coronation of George V in London.

Peuchen married when he was thirty-four, in 1893. He and his wife, Margaret, had two children, a boy and a girl.

His academic interests included chemistry and forestry. He was the first person in the British Empire to produce acetone directly from wood. The new chemical was an important constituent of the explosive cordite.

At age thirty-six, he formed a partnership with William MacKenzie to create the Standard Chemical Company of Canada. It took large orders from the Government of Britain for acetone. It also produced other much-sought-after chemicals such as methanol and formaldehyde.

Standard Chemical Company of Canada

As a result, Standard Chemical owned and operated lumber mills, factories and refineries in Canada and Europe. It became one of the most profitable businesses in both the Dominion of Canada and the Empire, and Peuchen became a wealthy man. His family lived in a fashionable mansion on Jarvis Street in downtown Toronto.

However, he spent most of his time at "Woodlands," the family's fifty-seven-acre country estate on the shore of Lake Simcoe north of the city, near Barrie. Built by timber baron Richard Powers in 1867, it had its own tennis courts, a golf course and a marina where Peuchen kept his yacht, *Vreda*.

Originally called "Beautiful Water" by the Huron Indians who lived there, Lake Simcoe became "the" place to be during the summer months for Toronto's elite. Today, it's the centre of Cottage Country.

Only nineteen miles (thirty kilometres) long and sixteen miles (twenty-six kilometres) wide, the relatively small, shallow, protected lake was popular with day sailors from Toronto's Royal Canadian Yacht Club, of which Peuchen was a member. In fact, he was elected vice commodore and rear commodore of the club.

Given his interest in new technology and his high social status, Peuchen was looking forward to sailing aboard *Titanic*. He convinced his good friend Harry Molson to make its maiden voyage with him. Molson was on Standard Chemical's board of directors, and both men had been in Europe on business.

On Sunday night, April 14, the two men had dinner together, along with a mutual friend from Montreal, Hudson Allison and his wife, Bess. After dinner, Peuchen stopped by the ship's first-class smoking lounge for a drink and cigar with several mutual friends, including Charles Hays, also from Montreal, and several gentlemen from out west.

Hugo Ross, thirty-six years old, was a real estate developer from Winnipeg. He was returning from a two-month trip touring the Mediterranean with a couple of bachelor friends, Thomson Beattie (also thirty-six) and Thomas McCaffry (age forty-six).

When Ross lived in Toronto, he often spent weekends crewing Peuchen's yacht. There, he had tried to make a go at being a stockbroker in Toronto, specializing in mining companies, but his firm, Fox and Ross, went bankrupt after a year.

He then headed north to the Klondike Gold Rush, hoping to make his fortune, but he was too late. By the time he arrived in 1902, the best claims had been bought up.

When his father, a former member of parliament, died, he inherited the family's fortune and returned to Winnipeg.

While in Egypt, Ross became ill, likely from dysentery, and the group of friends decided to cut their trip short. The three men had originally been booked on Cunard's *Mauritania*, but changed their reservations to *Titanic*. None of the three survived.

Ross was last seen by Arthur Peuchen near the ship's grand staircase, dressed only in his pajamas. When Peuchen told him that *Titanic* had hit an iceberg and that he should get dressed and go topside Ross replied, incredulously, "It will take more than an iceberg to get me off this ship."

Thomson Beattie did survive *Titanic*'s sinking initially. He was able to swim to the swamped lifeboat, Collapsible A, but he later died of exposure. The lifeboat had been stored on the roof of the officer's quarters on *Titanic*'s starboard side. Crewmen had been able to get it together, but weren't able to launch it before the ship took its death plunge — the lifeboat floated free when *Titanic* sank.

Approximately twenty individuals got in and either stood or kneeled in the freezing water inside. Others clung to its side. Shortly after dawn, Lifeboat Number 14, under the command of Fifth Officer Harold Lowe, found the mostly submerged collapsible lifeboat but only twelve individuals inside were alive.

Lowe left three dead bodies behind; one of these was Thomson Beattie. The derelict lifeboat drifted free and was not picked up until a month later, when the White Star liner *Oceanic II* came across it. The crew buried the remains of the three men at sea.

The body of Thomas McCaffry, the Vancouver branch manager of the Union Bank, was recovered a month later by the *Mackay-Bennett* out of Halifax. Since McCaffry had grown up in Quebec, it was sent on to Montreal, where it was interred in the Notre Dame des Neiges Cemetery. His granite headstone was paid for by his employer.

Peuchen escaped *Titanic* by volunteering aboard Lifeboat Number 6. The ship's second officer, Charles Lightoller, was in charge of loading lifeboats on the port side. He didn't allow male passengers in any of the boats, except for Peuchen.

Lightoller later told the U.S. Senate Committee that he had been shorthanded of sailors to put aboard the lifeboats under his charge. When Peuchen saw that Lifeboat Number 6 was undermanned he volunteered to help out. Lightoller asked Peuchen if he was a sailor, and Peuchen replied that he was a yachtsman. He then climbed out onto the davits holding the lifeboat, which had been partially lowered, and climbed down one of the ropes to the lifeboat below.

Lightoller described Peuchen as being a brave man.

Upon arriving in New York, Peuchen became an outspoken critic of Captain Smith, the *Titanic*'s crew and White Star president Bruce Ismay. He told several newspapers that both Smith and Ismay were criminally negligent for not heeding the warnings of icebergs ahead that had been received from other ships earlier in the day, and for *Titanic* going too fast.

"I cannot report too strongly that Mr. Ismay knew of the presence of icebergs, but deliberately took a chance," he told the Washington *Herald*.

As for Captain Edward Smith, Peuchen was even less kind with his comments. On his return to Canada, Peuchen told the Toronto *World*:

> *The loss of the* Titanic *was due to criminal carelessness in running at full speed through the ice with a new crew, despite the fact that he (Smith) had received repeated warnings by wireless of the vast ice field and bergs that lay in his path. Captain Smith, the one man, above all, who should have been at his post (that night), was quietly and leisurely partaking of a hearty dinner with a party of friends…had he been on the bridge, the horrible accident would have been averted.*
>
> *If ordinary caution or good seamanship had been used, the accident wouldn't have occurred.*

The Chicago *American* also quoted Peuchen as saying that there had been no lifeboat drills before the Sunday night of *Titanic*'s sinking, and that he was surprised there weren't enough crewmen to man each lifeboat.

> *If they were there, they were not at their station. I had supposed that there would have*

Vreda's bell

> *been a drill or something of the kind (earlier in the voyage), but I saw none. I judge it was what is called a "scratch crew," picked up for this voyage and unfamiliar with the boat* [Titanic], *even if sufficient in number.*

Because of his outspokenness and newfound notoriety, Peuchen was the only Canadian to testify at the U.S. Senate hearings in Washington, D.C. He did so on Tuesday, April 23, 1912.

There, he was also critical of the lifeboats. Most were not adequately prepared or supplied. His, Lifeboat Number 6, had its drain plug out. Had he not replaced it, the lifeboat would have quickly sunk, Peuchen said.

Nor was it equipped with any electric lamps or a compass. When onboard the *Carpathia*, he learned from other passengers that most of the other life-

Little Artifact, Big Significance

Lookout Frederick Fleet
Right: Key to Titanic's binoculars

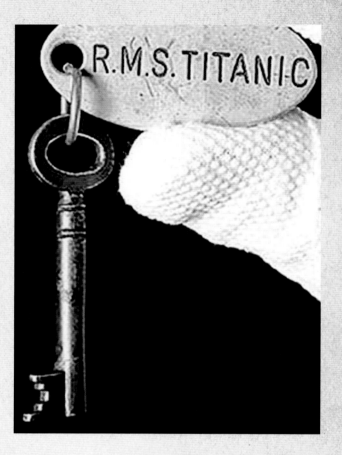

In the fall of 2007, an unusual artifact associated with *Titanic* went on the auction block in Wiltshire, England. It was the key for the box on the ship's bridge, where *Titanic*'s single pair of binoculars was stored.

It was accidentally left behind when the ship sailed from Southampton. The key was in the pocket of Second Officer David Blair, who had been transferred off *Titanic* to another White Star ship only a few days before.

Blair forgot he had the key until after the disaster. He kept it as a memento, and passed it down to his daughter, Nancy. She, in turn, donated it to the British & International Seamans Society in the 1980s, which put it up for sale with Henry Aldridge & Sons Auctioneers.

Bidding at the auction for the key was fierce. The one-of-a-kind item was sold to an anonymous buyer on the telephone for 90,000 pounds!

Frederick Fleet, one of *Titanic*'s lookouts, testified at the U.S. Senate Committee hearings held in Washington, D.C., several weeks after *Titanic* sank, that if he had being using the binoculars the night of the disaster they could have made all the difference.

"Well enough to get out of the way (of the iceberg)," he said.

Titanic's Telemotor

Titanic was actually steered by telemotor, though it's commonly known as the ship's wheel (or steering wheel).

The literal translation is "mover at a distance."

When the quartermaster (helmsman) turned the ship's wheel, a hydraulic cylinder in the telemotor caused a slave cylinder, which was powered by steam, to move in the steering engine located at the stern (rear) of the ship. This moved the steam valves on the engine, which responded by moving the ship's rudder.

A small double-acting, single-stroke pump at the telemotor kept the hydraulic system full of fluid. On *Titanic*, this was water mixed with glycerine. It was critical to keep the system warm so that the fluid would not freeze.

The pump's piston plunger forced the hydraulic fluid into one of two pipes that travelled the entire length of the ship, from the bridge to the steering engine. As the pressure in the line increased or decreased the valves on the steering engine opened and closed accordingly, moving the ship's rudder either to starboard (right) or to port (left).

Titanic's telemotor had a spring-loaded centring system that held the rudder in the position as indicated by the steering wheel (helm). The pump "clicked" when the steering wheel was turned one way or the other.

The quartermaster could check the accuracy of the ship's rudder position by looking at the redundant electrical rudder indicator located above the telemotor on the deckhead (ceiling).

If the quartermaster let go of the wheel it would not spin out of control, or return the ship's rudder to centre like some other, less advanced, steering systems of the time did. This was desirable on such a large ship. Otherwise, the quartermaster wouldn't have been able to hold the ship's wheel in position for very long. On such a big ship, he would have been fighting the ship's steering wheel constantly, causing him to steer a zigzag

Telemotor on the wreck

course. A large ocean-going ship, like *Titanic*, typically requires its rudder to be slightly at an angle most of the time in order to maintain a straight course.

When the wreck of *Titanic* was discovered in 1985, the only thing the occupants of the first submersible saw of the ship's bridge was its telemotor. The wooden superstructure of the bridge was long gone, eaten away by marine organisms.

Also gone was the rest of the bridge's gear — its engine telegraphs, its compass (in its binnacle), its telephones and all its other mechanical steering, navigation and communications equipment.

Since the wreck was discovered, subsequent expeditions to *Titanic* have laid artificial flowers and bronze plaques near the telemotor to pay their respects.

Engine room of the period

boats lacked essential survival supplies, like food rations and casks of drinking water. Some still had their sail aboard, while others did not.

He was also critical of the crewman in charge of Lifeboat Number 6, quartermaster Robert Hichens, whom he described as a "hardened sea lion" who was crude and rough with the women passengers.

Peuchen described Hichens as being unfit, and blamed him for steering towards what Hichens thought was a ship in the distance. Peuchen, instead, said that it was more likely a reflection on the water of, say, a bright star.

Hichens was the crewman at *Titanic*'s steering wheel on the bridge when it collided with the iceberg.

Peuchen seemed to be the single authority on *Titanic*'s sinking.

Ironically, Frederick Fleet, one of *Titanic*'s two lookouts, was also in Lifeboat Number 6. Peuchen said that Fleet had told him that he received no

confirmation from the bridge after he first spotted the iceberg and telephoned the bridge.

The man who rowed next to me in the lifeboat (Fleet) was the man on the crow's nest when the vessel struck. He said he had rung three bells on first seeing the iceberg, but had received no answer from the bridge (by telephone).

In addition to questioning *Titanic*'s chain of command and its efficiency of communication, Peuchen was also critical that the ship's lookouts had not been given binoculars.

If they had been, they would likely have seen the iceberg further off and the ship could have turned sooner to avoid it, he told the committee of senators.

His description of *Titanic*'s sinking and the events leading up to and following it were likely very accurate. He testified that the ship broke in two before it sank, when others did not. And, that it had been at a forty-five-degree angle when it was torn in two.

He had already told most of his story to the Toronto *World*, which had published it in its April 20th issue.

> *We heard an awful sound and a loud report boomed over the icy sea like an explosion. It was that the tremendous weight of the* Titanic *going down by the nose caused an air pressure in the centre amidships, and she broke in two, and foundered.*
>
> *Never have I heard such awful cries and shrieks. People came tumbling down like so many oranges. Chain, ropes, furniture and human beings were hurled in a terrible jumble into the sea, as if rolling down a steep hill.*

Also, Peuchen accurately estimated the amount of time a person could stand the frigid waters of the North Atlantic. He told the senate committee that the water's temperature was close to freezing and that no person could have lasted in it more than an hour.

At first, the know-it-all from Toronto was a hero, but the media quickly turned on him when more details surrounding the disaster became known. As the story about *Titanic* became legend, many of the facts were either downplayed or intentionally forgotten.

The most shocking statistic was that most of *Titanic*'s lifeboats had left half-empty and that they were mostly carrying first-class passengers.

For Peuchen, it became a case of people not wanting to believe what he said. The truth was too painful. Many simply dismissed him as being a liar; some argued that he only said what he did to make himself look good.

"He put himself in the position of a man who had to defend himself before the necessity for the defence was apparent," the Toronto *Mail* wrote.

Most of the public became suspicious of any male survivor, especially a first-class one. Peuchen was snubbed by Toronto high society, even though he had been called "a brave man" because of his efforts.

Innuendo and suspicion followed him for the rest of his days. One rumour had it that he had dressed as a woman to escape the sinking ship.

Things only got worse for him after World War I. Again, with such a great loss of life, the public was suspicious of any man who survived it, especially a military officer — even a reservist like Peuchen. But at fifty-five, he was far too old to have served overseas on the battlefield. Instead, he commanded the Home Battalion of the Queen's Own Rifles from Toronto.

After the war, Peuchen didn't spend much time in the city that had turned its back on him. He retired as the head of Standard Chemical and moved to Alberta, where he owned a ranch.

Like many of the era's wealthy, the 1920s hit Peuchen hard. He lost his fortune due to several bad investments. He returned to live in Toronto shortly before the stock market crash of 1929 — the start of the Great Depression.

Arthur Peuchen died on December 7, 1929, at the age of seventy.

In 1987, a Russian submersible recovered his wallet from *Titanic*'s debris field. He had left it behind in his first-class cabin on C Deck. In it was his calling card, some traveller's cheques and several streetcar tickets.

Titanic's Wireless

Radio was in its infancy when *Titanic* began its maiden voyage. Guglielmo Marconi had invented his "wireless" radio system for transatlantic communication only eleven years before but, by 1912, it was being used by most major shipping companies. The advantages of the system — being able to communicate with other ships at sea and with radio stations ashore — were obvious.

Transmitting a voice signal a major distance wasn't yet possible. Instead, Morse code, a communication system made up of electronic pulses (short "dots" and long "dashes"), was used.

The *Titanic* was first assigned the call sign MUC in January, 1912, but this was changed to MGY before the ship sailed on April 10. Call signs weren't standardized until the first International Radiotelegraph Conference, held in London on June 4 — after the ship sank. Prefixes were allocated on an international basis. English coastal stations and ships used the letters G or M as the first letter of their call sign. American stations and ships used the letters K, N and W. Germans used the letter D (for Deutsch), Italians the letter I, the French the letter F, and so on.

Dockside in Southampton, *Titanic*'s new Marconi wireless set was installed and operational by April 3, 1912. Its operators, Jack Philips (age twenty-five) and Harold Bride (age twenty-one), had exchanged messages with land-based stations as far away as around the Mediterranean. Captain Edward Smith had also sent several telegraphs to Bruce Ismay, managing director of the White Star Line, at the company's head office in London.

The wireless men weren't employees of the White Star Line, although their wages were paid by the shipping company. Their employer was the Marconi Company itself, which contracted its services to the various shipping lines and land stations that used its system.

Senior radio operator Jack Philips took the late watch (night shift) from 20:00 hours (8 p.m.) to 02:00 hours (2 a.m.). Deputy radio operator Harold Bride took the early watch from 02:00 hours (2 a.m.) to 08:00 hours (8 a.m.). During the daytime, the two men took turns at the wireless key, spelling off each other as necessary to sleep and eat. Regardless of the time, day or night, one of them was always at work.

Titanic's "Marconi room" was located on its boat deck behind the officers' quarters. It was a distance of approximately forty feet (thirteen metres) from the ship's bridge, connected via the corridor that ran down the port side of the forward superstructure.

The Marconi room was in the centre of the structure so it did not have a porthole. Natural light was provided from a skylight in the deckhead (ceiling) above. The operators' quarters were next door, on the starboard side, in a separate cabin. The men used the officers' washroom facilities across the corridor (on the port side).

The Marconi room was connected to the *Titanic*'s fifty-line telephone exchange but there was no telephone line connecting it with the ship's bridge. Messages concerning navigation, such as reports of icebergs received from other ships, were hand-delivered by the radio operator to the bridge directly. After the disaster, a speaking tube running from the Marconi room to the bridge was added on *Titanic*'s sister ships, *Olympic* and *Britannic*.

First- and second-class passengers could phone in the contents of their telegrams, or they could fill out a form at the Purser's Inquiry Office, located on the starboard side of the forward first-class entrance. The handwritten messages were paid for at the desk, at the rate of twelve shillings and sixpence for the first ten words, and nine pence per word after that. Telegram orders were sent to the Marconi room by pneumatic tube.

The duty man listened to incoming messages with his headphones and recorded incoming passenger

Marconi room

messages by hand. The messages were then typed on a telegram form by the other operator.

Messages were transmitted using the wireless's "key." It had a set of electrical contacts that moved when the key was depressed, which deactivated the receiver when transmitting. The key also had an emergency switch on its left side that could be used to break the circuit if the contacts became welded together by the high-voltage current.

The set's 1.5-kilowatt main spark transmitter was housed in an adjoining closed cabin to reduce the sound of its electrical "hum" and the smell of the ozone it produced. The system's magnetic detector, multiple tuner and spark coil were located in the Marconi room itself.

Both Philips and Bride remained at their station until the very end when *Titanic* foundered at 2:30 a.m. on Monday, April 15, 1912.

Bride, who survived, later said that he heard water flooding into the wheelhouse shortly before the great ship broke in two. Philips was in mid-transmission at the time, sending what was to be *Titanic*'s last radio call for help. He didn't survive.

Titanic – Technological Triumph and Tragedy

J. Bruce Ismay dreamed "big" when he first conceived *Titanic*. In fact, it was the second of three gigantic Olympic-class liners.

The Harland and Wolff Shipyard in Belfast, Ireland, got the order to build her at the end of April, 1907. Construction on the leviathan began two years later, commencing in early 1909. *Titanic*'s keel was laid on March 31 of that year.

Titanic was 882 feet (268 metres) long and ninety-two feet (thirty metres) wide. Her draft, the depth of water needed to float her, was thirty-five feet (eleven metres).

She had eight steel decks and a double bottom. She was fitted with two bilge keels amidship — each just under 300 feet (100 metres) long — that projected two feet (sixty centimetres) out on the sides of her hull. In addition to providing the ship with ballast, these also made it more stable, preventing her from rolling from side to side in a heavy sea.

In recent years, some *Titanic* historians and enthusiasts have theorized that steel from the bilge keels (damaged by the collision with the iceberg) may have punctured the ship's double bottom, making *Titanic* sink faster than it should have.

It took 3,000 workers two years to build *Titanic*. Two died in the process.

Twenty tons (eighteen metric tonnes) of rivets were used to construct her hull, which was made from a series of one-inch (two-centimetre) steel plates riveted together. Three million individual steel rivets were used.

For years, most experts thought that what caused *Titanic* to sink was a three-foot (one-metre) gash running three hundred feet (one hundred metres), starting near the bow and running along its starboard side — the result of the ship scraping alongside the iceberg (like a can opener opening the top of a tin can).

After the shipwreck was found in 1985, experts revised their position, believing instead that *Titanic* flooded because the steel plates on its starboard side had actually buckled on impact, causing them to separate from one another.

WEAK STEEL

Some experts also speculated that the steel used to make the rivets holding *Titanic*'s steel hull plates together was weak because it contained too much sulphur. The theory was largely dismissed, though, because the steel was also used for the rivets on White Star's two other Olympic-class liners, most notably the *Olympic*, "Old Reliable," which had a long and successful career. Rivets used to build other ships of the period were also shown to be similar in metallurgic composition. While the condition of the rivets may have been a contributing factor, it wasn't the sole cause for the ship taking on water.

Titanic's rudder weighed just over 100 tons (ninetey metric tonnes) and was made from six individual pieces because each was so heavy.

Ten pairs of draught horses were needed to pull the wagon carrying each of the great ship's two fifteen-ton (13.5–metric tonne) anchors from the foundry to the shipyard.

When fitted out, *Titanic* weighed just over 53,000 tons (forty-eight metric tonnes).

She was the equivalent in length to four city blocks. From her bridge to her keel she was as tall as a ten-story building.

She cost just over $400 million in today's money ($7.5 million in 1912) to build — the same cost, today, to build a Nimitz-class "super" aircraft carrier.

Even by today's standards *Titanic* was big: the *Queen Mary II*, which was launched in 2003, is only 231 feet (seventy-seven metres) longer.

STEAM POWER

Her two huge four-cylinder, triple-expansion reciprocat-

One of Titanic's *two anchors*

ing engines revolved seventy-seven times per minute, producing 15,000 horsepower each. These, in turn, were powered by the ship's twenty-nine Scotch boilers (twenty-four double-ended and five single-ended). Coal-fired furnaces heated the water in the huge boilers. Steam (at 215 psi/1.5 MPa) powered the two massive engines and *Titanic's* turbine engine. In addition to producing electricity for the ship, the state-of-the-art Parsons low-pressure turbine engine also propelled the ship's bronze quadruple-blade centre propeller, seventeen feet (5.5 metres) in diameter. The ship's two twenty-four-foot-wide (seven-metre-wide) bronze triple-blade propellers, located on the opposite sides of the centre propeller, were powered by the ship's two reciprocating engines.

Controlling the amount of steam fed to the engines controlled the speed of the ship. Titanic carried over 8,000 tons (7,300 metric tonnes) of coal in her bunkers and burned, on average, 825 tons (750 metric tonnes)

per day. Titanic's maximum speed was twenty-three to twenty-four knots.

Exhaust from the engines was vented through *Titanic's* first three funnels. Its fourth "dummy" funnel was used for ventilation and storage.

The low-pressure turbine also powered four four-hundred-kilowatt dynamos (generators) that produced a total of 16,000 amps of electricity at one hundred volts, which ran through 200 miles (320 kilometres) of electrical wire. In total, *Titanic* had approximately ten thousand electric lights, and each cabin was also equipped with an electric heater. There was a heated swimming pool for first-class passengers and there were four electric-powered elevators — three for first-class passengers and one for second-class passengers.

The Titanic also had a fully staffed medical "sick bay" with two doctors and an operating room.

There was even a fully equipped photographic dark room.

The **Titanic** *was called a triple screw steamer because of its three propellers.*

NOT WATERTIGHT

The transverse bulkheads divided *Titanic* into sixteen compartments, each made of half-inch (one-centimetre) steel plate. The ship's watertight bulkhead doors were held open by powerful electromagnets. In the event of an emergency such as a collision, simply flicking a switch on the bridge would lower them by cutting the power supply. On other ships of the period, bulkhead doors had to be lowered manually by using a crank mechanism located above each door. This took much longer than *Titanic's* new automated closing system.

Titanic could stay afloat with as many as four of its watertight compartments flooded. Unfortunately, the damage sustained from hitting the iceberg reached all the way into the ship's sixth compartment. It was only a matter of time before she sank.

By midnight, water in the damaged compartments began to spill over into the next, domino-like, because the top of each was only a few feet above the ship's waterline. By 1:20 a.m. water began flooding through the hawse-pipes (anchor-chain holes) at the ship's bow. By 2:10 a.m. the enormous weight of *Titanic's* stern caused the ship's bow to be completely underwater.

The stresses on the ship's midsection increased until finally it couldn't take any more. By this time, *Titanic* was at a forty-five-degree angle in the water. Experts estimate that the steel's breaking-point (stress at failure) was fifteen tons per square inch.

But it wasn't a clean break — the forward section of *Titanic*, now completely vertical under the surface, dangled from the stern section, continuing to drag it down for several minutes. When the bow part finally broke free, the stern portion righted itself and floated there for several more minutes. As it filled with water, it too raised high into the air, until it was almost vertical. Then it descended, sinking out of sight.

Some experts have concluded that if the ship's transverse bulkheads (the walls of the "watertight" compartments) had only been a few feet higher *Titanic* would have stayed afloat at least several more hours, enough time for the *Carpathia* and other ships to have reached her.

In fact, some experts have stated that *Titanic's* design actually contributed to its sinking because it kept the floodwater in the forward part of the ship.

After the disaster, the White Star Line modified its designs for future ships. Its other two Olympic-class ships, *Olympic* and *Britannic*, had their hulls modified — specifically, their transverse bulkheads were raised.

However, it wasn't until 1948, at the International Convention on Safety of Life at Sea, that a ship's hull design was standardized for increased safety, specifying the orientation, length, height and number of "watertight" compartments each passenger ship was supposed to have.

Elevators aboard Titanic

SMOKE DETECTORS

Titanic was one of the first ships to have a smoke detector system. The ship's master fire station was located near the bridge and was manned twenty-four hours a day, most of the time by the ship's lead fireman, Frederick Barrett (age twenty-eight).

The control panel was a set of glass tubes, which were connected to thin pipes running to different parts of the ship. A vacuum drew air back. A foil filament in each tube vibrated up and down, showing that the system was working.

If there was a fire in a particular area of the ship, smoke would eventually make its way up and into the corresponding glass tube on the control panel. The fireman on duty would then telephone the closest secondary fire station, which was also manned around the clock, to find out what the problem was. Fire hydrants and water hoses were strategically located throughout the ship for the ship's crew to use.

While most ships, and homes, of the day used iceboxes to keep food cold, the *Titanic* was equipped with large walk-in, thermostatically controlled refrigerators for each type of perishable food — meat, fish, fruits, vegetables, eggs and dairy products. There were also separate refrigerators for wines and spirits.

The *Titanic* was also fitted out with the latest in kitchen equipment, from the most advanced ovens of the day and steam tables for keeping food warm to stockpots. The floors in each of the ship's three galleys were also covered with specially-grooved tiles to provide better footing.

Some new appliances, like the "hot press" (used for making sauces) in the main galley, were acting up but, overall, everything was in fine working order on the ship's first trip out.

As baker Charles Burgess said, "Care and effort went into her. She was a wonderful ship."

TITANIC
The Future

Model of the Titanic *wreck from the* Titanic *Museum at Branson, Missouri*

"Finders keepers" is the rule when it comes to *Titanic*, but it comes at a price. RMS Titanic Inc. (RMST) battled courts in the U.S. for almost twenty years to gain title to more than three thousand artifacts it recovered from the famous shipwreck. Finally, in August 2011, a U.S. judge awarded ownership of the valuable artifacts to the company that recovered them.

After the *Titanic* wreck was discovered in 1985, Washington moved to make it illegal to own and sell artifacts from it within that country. In 1995, Canada, France and the United Kingdom joined with the U.S. in banning the sale of recovered artifacts, although the ruling does not prohibit the trade in artifacts from the ship in its day or artifacts that were recovered in 1912 at the site of the ship's sinking.

In 1993 a U.S. court declared RMST the custodian of the wreck, giving it the right to recover artifacts for the sole purposes of exhibition and education, but the artifacts were to remain public property. However, the terms of the agreement were not fully spelled out.

When the publicly traded RMST was struggling financially its top managers, at odds with both the company's shareholders and U.S. government regulators, wanted to sell the artifacts for a profit. The courts refused, and lawyers on both sides were busy for years negotiating a thick book of covenants and conditions.

In 2004, RMST's shares were bought up by Premier Exhibits, Inc., of Atlanta, Georgia, whose "Bodyworks" exhibits (of plasticized cadavers) have been seen around the world by millions of people. Premier has improved RMST's exhibition and marketing abilities — its travelling exhibition,

"*Titanic*: the Artifact Exhibition," has been seen in dozens of major cities worldwide, and there's a permanent exhibition at the Luxor Hotel in Las Vegas. In Canada, the travelling exhibit was most recently in Calgary, where it finished a five-month run in June 2011.

In 2007 RMST's new managers sought from the U.S. District Court a salvage award in the amount of $110 million — either as a payment of cash or an award of title to the artifacts — for its work in salvaging and conserving the artifacts recovered on multiple dives after 1987. Those artifacts, except the ones on display, are housed in the company's special temperature-controlled warehouse in Atlanta.

In 1993, a French court awarded RMST title to 1,800 artifacts, valued at $35 million fair market value, that were recovered in 1987 by RMST working in conjunction with the Institute of France for the Research and Exploration of the Sea (IFREMER).

As a sign of good faith, RMST embarked on a purely scientific expedition to *Titanic* in 2010, in co-operation with the Woods Hole Oceanographic Institution, the National Parks Service's Submerged Resources Center, the National Oceanic and Atmospheric Administration's National Marine Sanctuaries Program, the Institute of Nautical Archaeology and the Waitt Institute. The goal of that expedition was to map and film the two sections of the wreck and the debris field in between using the latest in underwater remote sensing technologies, including several state-of-the-art autonomous underwater vehicles. Some of the expected data and footage was destined to be used for new multimedia elements in an updated and redesigned *Titanic* artifacts exhibition, according to the company. Unfortunately, the trip was cut short due to bad weather.

Under the terms of the 2011 court decision, the 1987 and post-1987 artifact collections must be kept together as one single collection. Premier must also comply with provisions that will guarantee the long-term protection of the artifacts, and the company has already agreed to establish a preservation trust for the independent maintenance and conservation of the artifacts should the company go out of business. If RMST should sell its *Titanic* artifacts, the buyer would be subject to the same conditions applicable to Premier.

For now, the *Titanic*'s treasures appear to be properly cared for. As for the shipwreck itself, it will continue to erode. That is the nature of the tides and time. The wreck will continue to collapse in on itself. Parts of the ship have already declined considerably since it was discovered almost thirty years ago, especially the stern section. However, the bow section remains remarkably intact and will continue to be recognizable for many years to come.

What the future holds for the wreck and its contents is anyone's guess. One thing is for sure, the public's lust for all things *Titanic* isn't likely to die down any time soon.

Where to Go

Exhibit of Titanic *interior at the* Titanic *Museum Attractions in Pigeon Forge, Tennessee*

In addition to Premier's permanent *Titanic* artifacts exhibit in Las Vegas and the company's travelling exhibits, there are several other *Titanic*-dedicated museums in the United States that one can visit. *Titanic* Museum Attractions in Pigeon Forge, Tennessee, and Branson, Missouri, are actually half-scale models of the forward section of the famous liner. Inside, visitors can see reproductions of the *Titanic's* interior spaces and artifacts from the liner and other White Star ships of the period.

Many of the artifacts on display at both locations are on loan from collectors Tony and Ingrid Probst, who have one of the largest collections of Titanic artifacts in the world. Many of these were originally found at the surface where Titanic sank and were recovered by crewmen from the different rescue ships that were sent out to look for survivors and, later, victims.

In Canada, the Maritime Museum of the Atlantic in Halifax, Nova Scotia, also has a permanent *Titanic* exhibit. All of the *Titanic* artifacts on display there were also recovered in 1912 by crewmen aboard *Mackay-Bennett* and other ships. Over the years, the artifacts were donated to the museum, mostly by the descendants of those involved in the search for, and recovery of, *Titanic's* dead. Many of these victims were buried in Halifax's Fairview Cemetery.

Dubbed "the *Titanic* City," Halifax is also home to a number of other sites associated with the late great liner, including the residences of some *Titanic* passengers who were from the city. A walking tour of sites starts from the Maritime Museum of the Atlantic on Lower Water Street.

ACKNOWLEDGEMENTS

A book like this couldn't have been written without the help of many people. First of all, I would like to thank Jim Lorimer and Nancy Sewell from Formac for believing in both me and this project.

Next, I would like to thank my editor, Christen Thomas, editorial assistant, Chelsey Millen and Lindsey Hunnewell, the book's production coordinator, for their patience and professionalism.

My friend and colleague Dan Conlin, from the Maritime Museum of the Atlantic, helped this first-time author greatly with his knowledge and support. Thank you so much, Dan.

I'm also grateful to the many people I talked to over the past year who were either directly related to a *Titanic* passenger or who had knowledge about them. Some of these, like the good folks at the Nova Scotia Archives, were professionals; most were not. Thank you all for taking the time with me that you did.

Last, and most important, I want to thank, Beverley Ware. Without her, I wouldn't have written the book.

Rob Rondeau
October 2011
Lunenburg, Nova Scotia

NOTES ON SOURCES

If you would like to do further research about the *Titanic* and the passengers discussed in this book, there are a few key sources that were used as reference throughout *Titanic Lives*:

For general historical information about the ocean liner and its passengers, a few good resources are:

The *Encyclopedia Titanica* found at: www.encyclopedia-titanica.org; the Titanic Historical Society website: www.titanichistoricalsociety.net; and the online resource www.titanic-titanic.com.

Information on the White Star Line fleet of ocean liners as well as a list of *Titanic* passengers and crew can be found at www.titanic-whitestarships.com.

To learn more about Erickson's Workingman's club, Stewart Holbrook's "Elbow Bending with Giants" published by the Oregon Historical Society gives a clear picture of what a typical day visiting the saloon was like.

For detailed information on the Boer War, please see John Boileau's book *Canada's Soldiers in South Africa* (Halifax: Formac Publishing Company Limited, 2011).

If you want to learn more about William Ryerson specifically, visit the Eva Brook Donly Museum and Archives in Simcoe, Ontario.

Margaret Houghton's *The Hamiltonians* (Toronto: James Lorimer & Company Ltd., Publishers, 2003) is a good resource for finding out more information on Dr. Alfred Pain.

To learn more about the radio dispatch and technical issues surrounding the sinking of the *Titanic* see the *RMS Titanic and the Jack Phillips Story* by Glenn Dunstan of the Guildford & District Radio Society in the United Kingdom: http://gdrs.net/titanic/titanic%20radio%20page.htm and Vicki Bassett's article, "Causes and Effects of the Rapid Sinking of the *Titanic*" (Wisconson: College of Engineering, University of Wisconsin, 2000).

These other books that focus on the *Titanic's* story may also be of interest:

Don Lynch's and Ken Marschall's *Titanic: An Illustrated History* (New Jersey: Wellfleet Press, 2006); Alan Ruffman's *Titanic Remembered: The Unsinkable Ship and Halifax* (Halifax: Formac Publishing Company Limited, 2005); *Last Dinner on the Titanic: Menus and Recipes from the Great Liner* by Rick Archbold and Dana McCauley (Toronto: Madison Press Limited, 1997); and Judith Geller's *Titanic: The Artifacts Exhibition* (RMS Titanic, Inc., 2006).

PHOTO CREDITS

Bettman/Hulton Picture Library: p. 19 top; p. 94 left

Brown Brothers: p. 18

Canadian War Museum: p. 53 (CWM 19650036-003 George Metcalf Archival Collection)

China's News Service, China.com: p. 94 right

CPR Archives: p. 79 (NS12258)

Encyclopedia Titanica: p. 58 left, right; p. 68

Hudson Nieman Collection: p. 32

Images Ontario: p. 91

Library and Archives Canada: P. 47 left (C-005389); p. 47 right (PA-013413); p. 55

MacBride Museum of Yukon History collection: p. 46 (1991-4-20-62)

McCord Museum: p. 33 left

Mrs. John E. Ryerse: p. 56

National Library of Australia: p. 24 (Thomas Baines, "The Blue Jacket", an 4053991)

National Oceanic and Atmospheric Administration: p. 95

Nova Scotia Archives: p. 17 (NSA Photograph Collection: Transportation & Communication: Ships & Shipping: R.M.S. *Titanic* #1); p. 19 bottom (*The Sphere* (London, 27 April 1912), p. 72; NSA Newspaper Collection); p. 34 (NSA Fader Collection, 1972-21 no. 6); p. 35 (*The Sphere*, (London, 20 April 1912), p.52; NSA Newspaper Collection); p. 37 (*The Sphere* (London, 20 April 1912), p.49; NSA Newspaper Collection); p. 39 (*The Sphere* (London, 4 May 1912), p. 91; NSA Newspaper Collection); p. 41 (*The Sphere*: Supplement (London, 20 April 1912), p. ii; NSA Newspaper Collection); p. 64 (right, *The Sphere* (London, 4 May 1912), p. 99; NSA Newspaper Collection); p. 65 (*The Sphere* (London, 4 May 1912), p. vi; NSA Newspaper Collection); p.

66 (*The Sphere* (London, 20 April 1912), p. 63; NSA Newspaper Collection); p. 67 (*The Sphere* (London, 20 April 1912), p. 64; NSA Newspaper Collection); p. 74 (*The Sphere*: Supplement (London, 27 April 1912), p. 1; NSA Newspaper Collection); p. 75 (NSA Photograph Collection: Transportation & Communication: Ships & Shipping: R.M.S. *Titanic* #2)

Oregon Historical Society: p. 42 (Image Number 63169); p. 44 (Image Number 21750)

Private Collection of Alan Hustak: p. 10; p. 64 left

Private Collection of Betty Vanden Bosch: p. 33 right; p. 36

Private Collection of Bob Rutherford: p. 78; pp. 80-81

Private Collection of Harland and Wolff/ Ken Marschall: pp. 61-62; p. 96; pp. 102-103

Private Collection of Miles Collins: pp. 82-87

Private Collection of Rob Rondeau: p. 15, pp. 25-31; p. 45; pp. 48-51; p. 59; p. 101

Private Collection of Tony Probst: p. 38 top left, top right, bottom; p. 43 left; p. 89

Royal Canadian Yacht Club: p. 90; p. 93

Royal St. Lawrence Yacht Club: p. 72

Thomas A. Ryerson Collection: p. 52

Titanic Museum Attractions Branson, MO. & Pigeon Forge, TN, USA: p. 13; p. 43 right; p. 99; p. 104; p. 106

Ulster Folk and Transport Museum, Northern Ireland: p. 71

Wikipedia: p. 11, p. 16, p. 22; p. 73; p. 77

INDEX